FUNDAMENTALS OF PSYCHOLOGY

C. J. Adcock was born in England but reared on an 'out-back' farm in New Zealand where education was limited to a one-teacher school. He attended the Auckland Teachers' College and qualified as a primary-school teacher. He studied extramurally for his B.A., M.A., and Diploma of Social Science degrees. For several years he lectured on Psychology and Politics for the South-east District Workers' Education Association, England. He obtained his Ph.D. in London after the war, and returned to New Zealand to a university appointment in Wellington. He officially retired as Acting Professor in 1970 but continues some teaching and research in an honorary capacity. He became a Carnegie Fellow when he visited United States and European universities in 1954-5. He was also a visiting Professor at the University of Illinois in 1962 and during 1963 visited other universities in Europe, India, and Japan. He is a Fellow of the British Psychological Society and an Honorary Fellow of the New Zealand Psychological Society. He is President of the New Zealand Esperanto Association, and Vice-President of the Wellington Workers' Educational Association and of the New Zealand United Nations Association.

He has published *Problems of Life and Existence*, *Factorial Analysis for Non-mathematicians*, *Psychology and Nursing*, and numerous papers.

He is married to a psychologist and has two daughters by a former marriage.

C. J. ADCOCK

FUNDAMENTALS
OF
PSYCHOLOGY

WITH FOURTEEN TEXT FIGURES

PENGUIN BOOKS

PENGUIN BOOKS

Published by the Penguin Group
27 Wrights Lane, London W8 5TZ, England
Viking Penguin Inc., 40 West 23rd Street, New York, New York 10010, USA
Penguin Books Australia Ltd, Ringwood, Victoria, Australia
Penguin Books Canada Ltd, 2801 John Street, Markham, Ontario, Canada L3R 1B4
Penguin Books (NZ) Ltd, 182–190 Wairau Road, Auckland 10, New Zealand

Penguin Books Ltd, Registered Offices: Harmondsworth, Middlesex, England

First published by Price, Milburn & Co., New Zealand, 1959
First published in Great Britain by Methuen 1960
This revised edition published in Pelican Books 1964
13 15 17 19 20 18 16 14

Printed and bound in Great Britain by
Cox & Wyman Ltd, Reading
Set in Linotype Granjon

CONTENTS

EDITORIAL FOREWORD

SOME twenty-odd volumes have been published in the Pelican Psychology Series (together with other books on psychology not included in this series). For good and sufficient reasons it has not been possible before now to offer a general introductory text in this series on the subject as a whole. J. C. Flugel's *A Hundred Years of Psychology* (1933) contains a chapter on 'The Great Textbooks, Brentano to James'. The story should be brought up to date. A review of the textbooks of psychology would illuminate the history of psychology itself and its spectacular emergence as, next to atomic physics, the most important advance in science in the twentieth century. No one in this century can claim to be educated if he has not at least a nodding acquaintance with modern physics and with modern psychology.

At the turn of the century there were two authoritative texts: William James's *Principles of Psychology* (still preserved in part in Margaret Knight's Pelican, *William James*, A229) and G. F. Stout's *Manual of Psychology*. When psychology, early in the present century, became an established science (as distinct from a branch of philosophy) a different kind of text was needed. In England new texts were provided by William McDougall (*The Outline of Psychology*), by R. H. Thouless (*General and Social Psychology*), and by Rex and Margaret Knight (*A Modern Introduction to Psychology*). All these have passed through many editions.

In the United States there has been a remarkable succession of new textbooks including those by R. S. Woodworth, by N. L. Munn, and by E. R. Hilgard. Most of these texts underwent changes in successive editions. Earlier textbooks and earlier editions of the latter texts mostly presented the subject on the general plan of proceeding from the simpler to the more complex forms of experience and behaviour. Later textbooks and later editions of textbooks often reversed the order of exposition or experimented with other arrangements. There was no harm in this. In exploring a new world there are many places from which to set out and many possible routes of exploration.

This text, the *Fundamentals of Psychology*, can be commended to the reader as providing both a convenient point of departure and an interesting itinerary. Dr Adcock, who obtained his first degree and his doctorate at London University, has also studied and carried out research in the United States. He is accordingly well acquainted with, and sympathetic to, the approaches and the slants characteristic of British and American psychology. While sympathetic with many standpoints in psychology this book is not just eclectic. It aims at a synthesis. Recently, Dr Adcock has been engaged in research at Professor Raymond Cattell's laboratory at Illinois. Cattell's psychology is less well known in England than in the United States. It will be better known after the publication of a forthcoming Pelican written by Professor Cattell himself – for which Dr Adcock's *Fundamentals of Psychology* provides useful preliminary reading.

The reader who wishes to carry his studies further can proceed to some of the standard British and American textbooks, or to the more specialized volumes cited by the author or referred to in the end pages of this volume. Other suggestions for further reading will be found in the Psychology Section of the Penguin *Reader's Guide*.

This book can be commended not only to the general reader but also to young people still at school who may be proceeding to the university or to some other form of further education, and who contemplate a course of study such as psychology which is not included in the school curriculum. Teachers who encourage their pupils to explore subjects outside this curriculum can safely recommend this book as a sensible and readable account of what psychology is about.

C. A. MACE

PREFACE TO THE PELICAN EDITION

EARLIER editions of this book were designed primarily for students of psychology in universities. It has been revised with the general reader's interest in mind, but it is hoped that it will still be of use as an introductory text for students. The technical terms used are those which the serious reader needs to know. They are explained as introduced but, to facilitate reference, are also listed at the end of the book.

The book should serve as an introduction to a number of important psychological concepts presented here within a comprehensive, integrated *schema* so that the reader should be able to see psychology as a unified science. For the general reader, faced with a plethora of popular books on the subject, it is hoped that this one will provide an insight into the basic principles of scientific psychology. For the college student it offers, within one small volume, a comprehensive grasp of the field as a whole which may easily be lost in the detailed exposition of larger texts.

The stress throughout is on systematization and, while this is based upon an eclectic approach ranging from neurology to psycho-analysis, no attempt has been made to cover the contributions of all schools of thought. That can come later. For the beginner a well integrated conceptual *schema* must have priority. He will want later to amend it in various ways in the light of more advanced reading but before he strides out for himself he should stand on firm ground. If the book omitted all controversial concepts there would be nothing to unify, but to include all possible conflicting views would cause confusion and bewilderment.

The author also hopes that the systematization of the subject, while presented in terms appropriate for the lay reader and the beginner, may also prove of interest in its theoretical implications to the more advanced student of psychology.

C. J. A.

Acknowledgements are due to the following for permission to use illustrative material: McGraw-Hill Book Co., Inc., for Figure 1, from *Physiological Psychology* by Morgan and Stellar; Figure 4, after Jastrow; James Nisbet and Cambridge University Press for Figure 6, from Spearman's *Creative Mind*; Institute for Associated Research for Figure 7, from *Human Behaviour from the Transactional Point of View* by Franklyn K. Kilpatrick; M. B. King for Figure 13 (photograph).

SECTION ONE

INTRODUCTION

WHAT IS PSYCHOLOGY?

REFERENCES to psychology in the daily press and in popular periodicals are now numerous, but the variety of ideas as to the nature of psychology is correspondingly extensive. The most popular notion is that psychology is concerned in some way with the study of the mind. This accords with the derivation of the word, the Greek root of which refers to mind or soul. This is also substantially the definition given by the *Concise Oxford Dictionary*, but psychologists themselves prefer to avoid any assumption about the nature of the mind. Most of them would prefer a definition in terms of behaviour rather than of mind. Behaviour is objective and observable; mind is an assumption and, even if a justifiable assumption, not the primary object of our study.

The existence of so many varied conceptions of the nature of psychology is no doubt related to the many aspects of psychological work. The psychiatrist coping with 'mental' breakdown, the educator moulding human development, the vocational counsellor advising on the choice of jobs, the social scientist studying the prevention of crime, the personnel manager smoothing human relations in industry, the industrial psychologist streamlining industrial processes to suit the nature of human capacities: all these are concerned with psychology. Human behaviour is complex and varied, and the science which studies it must have many aspects. It may be useful for us to consider samples of psychological work in various areas.

A SIMPLE INDUSTRIAL PROBLEM

A large London catering firm became concerned about the

excessive number of breakages by its employees. It therefore decided to impose a penalty to reduce carelessness. Strange to say, the system of fines led to an *increase* in breakages. Such is the perversity of human nature. The management decided the problem was more complex than they had thought, so they called in a psychologist to investigate and recommend appropriate remedies. The psychologist first posed the question as to when breakages occurred. He kept a record of the breakages occurring during half-hour periods over a number of days, and it soon became evident that most accidents occurred during the rush periods when the girls were worried by their inability to cope with the number of orders. It was now obvious why the system of fines had only made matters worse. They added to the anxiety of the already over-taxed girls and simply made them more nervous.

A CASE OF PHOBIA

A *phobia* is an abnormal fear. Often the feared thing is quite harmless and the victim knows this, but he cannot reason with himself about it and just feels intensely afraid. Bagby tells of a young woman who had been troubled by such a phobia since she was seven years of age. She could not bear the sound or sight of running water. On one occasion she fainted at school because of the sound of the drinking fountain. Any suggestion of running water was sufficient to give her a severe fright.

The explanation of this condition lay in an experience which she had in her seventh year. She had been taken for a picnic with her mother and her aunt and had remained behind with her aunt after her mother had to return home. Forgetting her promise to obey her aunt, she ran away alone in the woods and was later found by her aunt wedged between two rocks of a small stream with water splashing over her head. Her fright can easily be imagined, but added to this was anxiety about her mother's reaction to her escapade. The aunt promised to say nothing of the incident and did not revisit the family for thirteen years. In the meantime the girl had developed her phobia. When the aunt returned and learned of the position she told the story. The recall of the incident was the crucial point in the patient's cure. Her unreasoning fear disappeared.

READING DIALS

The handling of modern aircraft places a severe strain on the pilot who must deal with many things in rapid succession. He is called to keep watch on a number of dials which give him vital information about his speed, altitude, the state of his engines, etc. It is essential that these dials should be easily read and not subject to error. What form should they take? They may have vertical scales or horizontal scales, they may be semicircular or completely round. The whole scale may be visible or only part through a small window. Only careful trials with a number of observers can establish which is the preferred form. Sleight conducted some research to discover the best form for such dials and found that the open-window type is the best. This seems reasonable since only a part of the scale appears in the window, and so there is less effort called for to read the precise point on the scale, but the psychologist has learned never to trust reasoning of this kind. Reasoning may suggest the answer but always *we must try it out*.

DISTRIBUTION OF LEARNING PERIODS

If you have to learn a skill or commit something to memory the question arises as to whether you should complete the job in one sitting ('strike while the iron's hot'), or whether it is better to spread the learning over a number of periods ('let it sink in'). A number of experiments have been carried out to decide this matter and, although results vary according to specific circumstances, the general trend is quite definite. In one of these investigations two similar groups of subjects were set to memorize material. The first group read through the material sixteen times in one day. The other group also read through the material sixteen times but spread the readings over sixteen days at the rate of one per day. Each group was tested a fortnight after completion of the learning to see how much had been retained. The results showed a startling difference. The first group remembered nine per cent of the material while the second group remembered seventy-nine per cent despite the fact that there was so much opportunity to forget during the sixteen-day period of learning. We shall comment on this later (see Chapter 7).

WHY DO WE FORGET?

It is customary to blame forgetting on a bad memory and there is no doubt that people do differ considerably in their innate capacity to remember things, but Freud has brought to our notice another aspect which is most interesting. In effect he says that we forget because we want to do so. One may retort that it is unfortunately just the things one wants to forget which insist on remaining vividly in our memories. A good instance is in an ancient formula for changing lead into gold. The process is a somewhat complicated one, but the crucial part requires that we run round a churchyard three times at midnight and not once during the period think of the word abracadabra. The process is quite certain, we are assured, if we carry out the instructions precisely. Of course abracadabra refuses to remain out of our thoughts and so we fail.

But this is not quite what Freud meant. He gives a neat example from his own experience. On considering the appointments which he had forgotten to keep he discovered that they were all for patients who were not being charged a fee! We all have the experience of forgetting to answer letters and usually we must admit that we didn't want to answer the letter. If a letter is likely to bring a cheque or some specially welcome news in return we seldom forget. Further discussion of this and other factors involved in forgetting we must defer to the appropriate chapter (Chapter 7).

SOCIAL PROBLEMS

During the Second World War food supplies became a pressing problem and in many countries food had to be rationed. In the United States of America, where the position was not so acute, some interesting social research was triggered off. Kurt Lewin (then director of the Research Center for Group Dynamics) and his associates posed themselves the problem of how to change people's eating habits by psychological forms of persuasion.

The first step was to determine who were the key persons in controlling eating habits. Housewives, it was decided, play a vital role here. They are in an excellent position to initiate the trial of new foods and generally influence consumption habits. An experiment was therefore set up to discover the most effective way of modifying their behaviour. Red Cross groups, formed for the study of nursing and first aid, provided convenient samples of housewives for the experiment. These women were all seriously concerned with the war effort and likely to be sympathetic to the aims of the experiment.

Six groups were chosen. Three of these received carefully prepared lectures designed to interest them in the merits of less favoured forms of meat such as hearts and kidneys.

These lectures were delivered by women who were able to speak not only about the nutritional qualities of the meats concerned but also of their own success in preparing attractive dishes from them for their own families. The other three groups were given similar information but in the form of discussions which were concluded by asking how many housewives would be prepared to try out these foods during the coming week.

The response to this appeal was excellent but it was in the actual behaviour of the women afterwards that the most striking effect was observed. Of the women in the first three groups who had heard the lectures only, the number who actually tried the proposed dishes was three per cent; but thirty-two per cent of the members of the other three groups, those who had actively participated in discussion and made a group decision, responded in a practical way. The second approach was thus more than ten times as effective. Further experiments gave similar results and indicated that a sound technique had been discovered.

During the last war careful psychological studies were also made of enemy peoples so that their behaviour could be better understood and predicted. This was extremely useful with regard to the use of propaganda which played quite an appreciable part in deciding the outcome of the war. But similar studies could be equally useful during peacetime in helping us to understand other nations better and so to get along better with them. Nothing is so prolific of conflict as misunderstanding, and only those who have made careful studies of other peoples can realize just what opportunities there are for misunderstanding. For example, we all appreciate what is meant when someone pokes out his tongue at us. We therefore completely fail to understand the behaviour of the Chinese, who pokes out his tongue to express innocent surprise. This is a superficial example but highly indicative.

PREDICTING BEHAVIOUR

A practical test of any science is its ability to predict. The astronomer can predict precisely when an eclipse is going to occur, and can do this a hundred years in advance. The psychologist can never hope to approach this level of ability. His material is too variable, but from time to time he is called on to predict and is not without success in this area. (It should be noted, however, that there are examples from the physical and natural sciences of difficult prediction because of the complexity of the data, e.g. oceanography and meteorology. Psychology is not unique in this respect.) Some very interesting examples occurred during the war when it was important that the government should have some idea how the public would respond to measures of national importance. In the U.S.A. psychological help was often invoked under these circumstances.

In 1942 the U.S. Treasury was considering the imposition of a special 'victory tax' which was to be deducted directly from wages. A complication arose because a campaign had been conducted to persuade wage-earners to buy war loan on a deduction-from-wages plan. The question was what would happen to this system if direct taxation on wages were instituted. Would wage-earners now decide they were paying enough directly out of wages and no longer wish to continue their purchase of war loan? Or would the war-loan scheme be unaffected? A psychological research survey was conducted which involved careful interviewing of a selected sample of the population. The conclusion was that there would be no interference provided the tax was introduced to the workers in a suitable way. The tax was instituted and the recommendation of the psychologists as to the method of introduction was followed. The prediction was completely verified, there being no detectable reduction in war-bond buying out of wages.

The above examples have been chosen to indicate the kind and diversity of psychological work. They represent isolated samples of behaviour. Our task in the succeeding chapters will be to build up a systematic knowledge of the human being as a behaving organism. We need to know not little odd scraps of unrelated knowledge, but to know how these fit together. One may have learned with regard to one's motor-car that it sometimes refuses to go after being out in the rain, that a broken wire causes similar effects or that the failure of the battery is equally incapacitating, but, if one understands the function of electricity as the basis of the ignition system, all these disturbances are seen as having a common element and their effects could be predicted although one had never previously experienced them. Furthermore, one then is in a much more effective position to apply appropriate remedies, or to recognize the infinite variety of similar defects such as a blown fuse, a wire touching the engine, a sticky cut-out or a dirty sparking-plug.

It is this breadth of knowledge which we wish to get of the human being. We need to know his structure and the principles on which he works. Does electricity or chemistry play any part in his functioning? Has he any batteries to run down? Has he brakes or any system of controls? On what basis can we predict his behaviour? Will the principles which explain the operation of the motor-car or the radio set explain his behaviour, too, or must we invoke further principles not recognized by physicist or chemist?

SECTION TWO
PRIMARY SOURCES OF
BEHAVIOUR

2

THE REFLEX SYSTEM

We have defined the subject-matter of psychology as behaviour. We shall begin our study by considering how we come to behave at all. Some of the earlier discussions in psychology assumed that man was a 'rational creature' whose behaviour could be accounted for in terms of common-sense reasoning. Modern psychology has found this to be far from the truth. Certainly man reasons, and the study of reasoning processes is an important part of psychology, but reasoning explains only a small part of behaviour. Before reasoning can have any significance there must be motivation of some kind. There must be something to push the organism into action, some dynamic. The steering mechanism of a car is of no use unless the engine is running and the car is in gear. In human beings, reasoning is only part of the steering mechanism.

There are two primary sources of behaviour in the more complex biological organisms, which include men. The simplest form is the reflex which we shall consider in some detail in this chapter. This is a rather stereotyped form of response which could be duplicated by an electronic mechanism. Much more complicated forms of behaviour are mediated by a much more flexible system which results in varied forms of striving until the related need has been met. Such a mechanism is known as a 'drive' and the most widely recognized drives are described in Chapters 3 to 5.

Reflexes and drives are the primary sources of our behaviour but any explanation of adult behaviour must also take into account the effects of learning. Both reflexes and drives become modified by experience. The principles underlying this and the specific ways in which learning results in the development of personality and abilities are treated in later chapters. All this gives insight into the most complex forms of behaviour, those which involve what is commonly called *volition*.

The present chapter is concerned with the simplest kind of response behaviour, the most primitive source of activity. In some respects it is a physiological mechanism rather than a psychological mechanism, but it is a source of behaviour and it has principles in common with more complex behaviour.

Much of human behaviour is highly complex, difficult to predict or even to explain after it has taken place, but some elements in our behaviour are surprisingly stable and it is these which we shall now consider. As an example let us take the simple withdrawal reflex. Take a spoon from a hot cup of tea and place it unexpectedly on the hand of a friend. The response takes place before the victim has time to think of what is happening to him and is quite involuntary. Responses such as this are dependent upon pre-formed neurological connexions and many of them function independently of the brain. If the spinal cord of the dog is cut just below the brain so that no nerve impulses can reach the brain it will still make a withdrawal response if its paw is pinched.

The net of neurological connexions responsible for a simple response of this kind is known as a *reflex arc*. It is customary to think of a reflex arc as consisting of three nerve units or neurons: a sensory neuron which brings in a nerve impulse (e.g. from the skin), a connecting neuron in the spinal cord and a motor neuron which conducts the nerve impulse out to a muscle (i.e. 'reflects' the impulse). This, however, is rather an over-simplification, certainly so far as the more complex reflexes are concerned. Before going further into this let us pause for a moment to consider what a neuron is and how the nerve conducts.

A neuron consists of a single nerve cell and may take many forms, one of which is shown in the accompanying diagram, but all consist of a central cell body which lengthens out into a long fibre (as much as several feet in some cases) and ends in fine branches. The other end of the cell body branches immediately into a fine network known as dendrites or dendrons. A nerve consists of a bundle of such neurons enclosed within a protective sheath except when they enter within the brain. The axon of one neuron branches within the dendrons of others so that it may pass on its impulse to any one of perhaps hundreds of other neurons with whose dendrons it has contact.

The point of contact between an axon and a dendron is known as a *synapse* and it is the relative amount of resistance at the various synapses which determines the route of the nerve impulse. Conduction through the synapse is relatively slow and may require as much time as the traversing of the complete neuron. Hence responses which are mediated through several synapses may be considerably delayed. The simple reflex is thus a very rapid response. In fact some of the reflex responses are just about ten times as fast as the quickest voluntary action, e.g. pressing a telegraph key on a given signal.

NERVE CURRENTS

We have talked glibly about nerve conduction. It is about time we gave some thought to the nature of the nerve impulses. Are they like electrical currents? As a matter of fact there is an actual transmission of electricity, but it does not travel as along an electric cable. Electricity normally travels at the rate of 186,000 miles per second, but nerve conduction is very much slower, reaching about 130 yards per second, less than a quarter of the best effort of a jet plane! But although nerve conduction is slow it has one decided advantage over the ordinary conduction of electricity; the current loses none of its strength. The process is like fire travelling along a trail of gunpowder where the gunpowder continually renews the energy. The gunpowder trail of course can function only once and then has to be renewed. Fortunately nerves do not have to be renewed each time they are used, but there is something analogous to renewal.

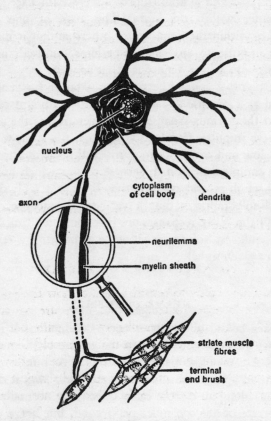

nucleus

cytoplasm of cell body

axon

dendrite

neurilemma

myelin sheath

striate muscle fibres

terminal end brush

Fig. 1. The neuron.

A chemical process is required before the nerve is ready again to conduct, and this chemical process requires oxygen.

We have spoken of an actual transmission of electricity along the nerve. This is not strictly true. What really happens is that each part of the nerve in turn becomes 'electrified', this area, about 40 mm. in length, passing along the nerve and producing the same effect as an electric current, just as a wave coming in on the beach seems to involve the actual travelling along of the water. Instruments, however, record an electrical effect of about one twentieth of a volt.

Another important effect of this method of nerve conduction is that conduction can only be in successive waves with a break between while the nerve recovers. This break is known as the *refractory period* and lasts a little less than half a thousandth of a second (known as a millisecond).*
Now since the strength of a nerve current is always the same the magnitude of the effect can be varied only by having more impulses travelling in a given time or by having more neurons involved. Both of these means are important. A single impulse is insufficient to pass a synapse. Summation of impulses by one or both of the above means breaks down the synaptic resistance.

NATURE OF THE REFLEX

We are now ready to consider further how the reflex operates. We have to remember that there are no absolutely closed circuits in the nervous system, with one receptor wired directly to an effector (usually a muscle) like a private telephone system, but rather some preferred pathways. The nerve impulse which produces even the simplest reflex response does not merely 'reflect' back to the muscle, but

---

* There is a much longer period when conduction is below normal. This is a minor exception to the all-or-none principle of conduction.

stimulates many other parts of the nervous system so that response can take place at various levels and with varying degrees of complexity. The stimulus may merit conscious attention or simple reflex response may be sufficient, as when we brush off a fly during the course of our reading.

The complicated nature of the interconnexions of the reflex system is revealed by a consideration of what happens when we step on a tack. The response is by no means the contraction of a single muscle. All the major muscles of the body must make the appropriate adjustment to keep us balanced despite the violent withdrawal. If we had consciously to will each muscle to contract to the requisite degree we should be faced with the sort of problem which would keep an engineer occupied for a long time with his slide rule. Our reflex system, however, takes charge of the situation and neatly coordinates our action.

Reflexes in various forms take care of a large proportion of bodily activity of a routine nature and so leave us free to concentrate on the more difficult problems of living. A brief survey of some of these areas of reflex activity will clear the ground for our further discussions. We have referred in the previous paragraph to a group of reflexes known as the *locomotor and postural reflexes*. Merely to stand still requires a complex set of coordinations. This is achieved through a system which is largely under the control of balance registering mechanism in the inner ear. This consists of three semicircular tubes ('canals') arranged to operate like carpenter's levels, one registering in the horizontal plane, one in the vertical left–right plane and one in the vertical front–back plane. These give us full information about our movements in the three dimensions and the reflexes automatically correct our balance in terms of this information. Some animals are able to walk almost immediately after birth, and although a little wobbly at first are able to locomote satisfactorily in terms of their reflex systems. Babies have to learn to walk, but this is largely because of physiological immaturity. If they are prevented from attempting to walk until they are sufficiently mature the period of learning is very short, but their progress is appreciably slower than that of animals which learn immediately after birth. Perhaps one should allow for the greater difficulty of balancing on two legs, though!

Cats notoriously always fall upon their feet and this is due to a *righting* reflex which operates in the same way as our own balancing mechanism. If the semicircular canals are not functioning the cat can still right itself in terms of visual cues, but if it is also blindfolded it fails to fall on its feet. In the same way human beings whose labyrinths (semicircular canals) have been damaged by disease can still keep upright provided they can see, but as soon as they find themselves in the dark they collapse.

A group of *digestive reflexes* takes care of our food and is responsible for the secretion of appropriate digestive juices at the right moment and for muscular movements which cause the digesting food to move through the digestive system as each stage in the process is completed. The original intake of food is also dependent on reflexes. Sucking is a reflex response which takes place automatically when babies or young animals make contact with a suitable object. Swallowing is also a reflex and involves a series of muscular contractions which propel food through the oesophagus.

The withdrawal reflex which we discussed earlier is one of a large group of *defensive reflexes* which include blinking, scratching, coughing, sneezing, and vomiting. Blinking obviously aims at protecting the eye from injurious objects. Recent experiments have suggested that this is a learned response, but it certainly becomes operative at an early age and is commonly accepted as a typical reflex. Further research will establish whether or not it is innate and so a true reflex. Coughing and sneezing are designed to remove foreign objects from the throat and nose respectively. When we say we 'have a cough' we mean that we have a chronic irritation in the throat which provokes repeated coughing in an effort to expel it. Vomiting in a similar way expels foreign objects from the stomach. It is, however, not so discerning as some of the other reflexes and will often operate at the wrong time!

A special group of defensive reflexes is that embodied in the so-called *nocifensor system*. This consists of a network of nerves which are responsible for the local defence of tissues against injury. If a small area of skin is damaged there is a reddening at the point of contact, and this, with an accompanying heightened tenderness, tends to spread slowly into the surrounding areas for ten to twenty minutes. The effect may last for some hours and results in careful protection of the injured part while the repair processes are initiated.

The *tendon reflexes* appear to serve no useful purpose outside the doctor's surgery. He makes extensive use of them to provide information about the functioning of the nervous system. In case of injury to the spinal cord the presence or absence of various tendon reflexes will indicate the location of the damage. These reflexes are elicited by tapping the tendons where they are accessible to surface pressure. The sudden tension on the tendon is transmitted to the muscle which will usually respond with a violent contraction. Thus a tap just below the kneecap when the leg is hanging freely will cause the latter suddenly to jerk outwards. This is the well-known knee-jerk or patella reflex.

Another group of reflexes appears to have chiefly social value. These might be termed the *expressive reflexes* since they indicate the experiences of the person making them. Groaning, smiling, weeping, wincing, and scowling are examples of this group. They appear to represent a primitive sort of language and serve to communicate elemental facts to other people. During certain stages of development they may be very important. Crying is the chief means by which the baby is able to call attention to his wants. Animals, which have no language in the human sense, may still achieve certain language functions by means of reflex types of response. The clucking of the hen keeps her chicks in contact with the group. Some birds have distress calls which warn other birds of danger, and so on.

Some reflexes are associated with our sense organs. There is a muscle in the ear which increases our hearing sensitivity when we listen attentively. A well known reflex controls the admission of light to the eye, the pupillary reflex. This is very obvious in the cat whose eyes seem to be narrowed to a tiny slit in bright sunlight but are wide open in the dark. If you cover a friend's eyes so as to keep out the light and then suddenly uncover them you will be able to see the pupil obviously contracting. This response is used by the doctor as a means of checking on the depth of coma when a person faints, since the reflex is absent in deep coma.

Finally we should refer to a series of reflexes which are concerned to regulate vital physiological functions. Temperature regulation is taken care of in this way so that there is very little variation of body temperature except in disease. Heartbeat and breathing are similarly controlled. Most of these reflexes are of little direct interest to the psychologist, but some of them can be utilized to throw light on psychological changes as in the case of the so-called lie detector.

CONTROL OF REFLEXES

Can we consciously control a reflex? Obviously some at least cannot be controlled since they operate without our knowledge. We have no consciousness of the changes in size of our pupils unless we observe our eyes in a mirror. In other cases we are aware of the response but not until after it takes place, as in the case of withdrawal reflexes. Here again it would appear to be impossible to control, since we do not know in time to do anything about it. It is possible, however, that if we anticipate the stimulus we can fortify ourselves against it. The hot-spoon stimulus in our first example may be quite ineffective if the victim notices what is happening. The degree of control varies considerably. An interesting case occurs with regard to wrist movements. Where the wrist has been injured so that all the tendons on one side have been damaged and the wrist consequently is bent permanently in one direction, it is possible to reverse some of the remaining tendons in order to bring about a balance. The patient soon learns to control the movements of his wrist in the normal manner and can bend his wrist backwards and forwards at will. When, however, he attempts to move one finger relative to another he loses control of the wrist because now the wrist muscles revert to reflex control and are no longer subject to his conscious willing.

3

DRIVES AND NEEDS

WE have just been considering responses which involve specific patterns of muscular movements. These responses are of a relatively simple nature and can be inherited as a unit by the organism. We have now to consider some situations which cannot be dealt with in this cut-and-dried manner. If food could always be had simply by reaching for it we should doubtless have a simple food-reaching reflex, but food is not always easily obtained and may require different tactics at different times. It is, however, essential that we should satisfy our food needs and this is attained by means of what is now usually referred to as a *drive*. The drive towards obtaining food is what we call *hunger*. When we are hungry all attention tends to be directed towards the obtaining of food. We are restless and dissatisfied until we get food. Our intelligence, our abilities, and all our past experience are mobilized to this end.

It will be obvious that drives are highly appropriate to the purpose which they service. They are flexible and yet persistent. Under very varied conditions they still lead to the satisfaction of the need. This is a matter that we must get quite clear. Reflexes operate at the level of mechanism. Although they can handle some extremely complex action they do so in the way that we might expect of an automaton. Engineers have in recent times achieved marvels in the way of complicated machines and there seems little that is outside the scope of the future automata. Complex skills, the solving of difficult logical problems, the working out of abstruse mathematical equations, playing a complicated game like chess: all this is within the scope of automata.

Let us consider just how much is possible from an automaton. There is no reason why one should not be designed to reproduce the activities of an average man. It could wait for the bus to take it to work in the morning, climb aboard the bus, get out at the factory, and proceed to control the activity of a machine. It could take its meals at appropriate times, could sit by the fire in the evening and smoke a pipe. Finally it could retire to bed. None of these tasks is intrinsically impossible to an automaton. But if an automaton did all these things how would it differ essentially from a human being? Most people who have tried to answer this type of question have done so in terms of *thinking*, but in a sense the automaton can think (we talk of electronic brain); what the automaton cannot do, and what no one has ever claimed it might ever do, is to *feel*. The automaton has no feelings, and we cannot conceive of it ever having any. It may behave as a human being behaves when hungry but it would not *feel* hungry.

This ability of organisms, and particularly human beings, to feel, to experience pleasure and pain, to be happy or sad, to hate or to love, distinguishes them sharply from all mechanical, chemical, or electrical systems. What is more, it makes them vastly more efficient. Something analogous to their purposeful striving can be built into an automaton, but the purpose is always one imposed by the designer and achievement of the purpose has to be within a reference frame also dependent on the designer. The chess-playing automaton 'strives' for victory in the game but operates only within the rules of the game. It cannot play poker nor can it deal with an opponent who makes an illegal move or smashes some of its valves. It cannot leave the game to rescue itself from a sinking ship.

DRIVE AND NEED

We shall again take up the question of the flexibility and efficiency of the human organism when we discuss learning. At this stage we are more concerned to be clear about the actual nature of drives. A distinction between drive and need may be of some help here. The hunger drive is related to the need for food. Some psychologists have spoken as though human behaviour could be explained in terms of needs. If one understands by need what we have here termed a 'drive' (and Tolman, one leading psychologist, has used the word in this way), no doubt it is true. But if we understand *need* in its ordinary sense as something necessary for a particular purpose, it is certainly not true. Food may be necessary to a human being in the sense that without it he cannot survive. It does not follow that he will do anything about it. Doctors are familiar with a malady which leads the patient to refuse all food although quite aware that food is essential to existence. An organism will satisfy its needs only in so far as the necessary action is automatically cared for by reflexes or in so far as it has a drive to this end. To assume that a person will seek food because food is necessary to life is to make the further assumption that the person wishes to live, i.e. that there is a drive towards self-preservation. This is, of course, true of most people, but we must not lose sight of the fact that we *are* explaining behaviour here in terms of drive and not just in terms of need. Need alone cannot move to action. Furthermore we must not make the mistake of thinking that people eat because of the need for food in preserving life. The average person eats because he *likes* it, because it satisfies a drive.

We are here stressing something which has been rather overlooked by many psychologists who have, in recent times, been unduly influenced by the attempt to explain all behaviour in terms of the principles of chemistry and physics. A consideration of the history of psychology throws some light on the origin of this tendency. A strong motive has been the desire to attain scientific respectability. But no science can just take over the models of other sciences. It must explain in terms of the principles which are most effective in its own field, only taking care that these do not conflict with the findings of other sciences.

TWO KINDS OF EXPLANATION

Let us consider some of the unique requirements in psychology. People often ask the question: 'Why?' Most sciences are busy answering this question. Let us point out two kinds of answer which can be given. Children ask, 'Why does it rain?' Most parents can explain about evaporation and condensation, but notice that, in a sense, this tells us not why it rains but *how* rain comes about. So far as rain is concerned this is the appropriate sort of answer, but it does not follow that we should always understand the question *why* in this sense. 'Why did you eat the peach?' may be much better answered in terms of 'I like eating peaches'. Strictly, *why* assumes a purpose. We can have no truck with motives in physical sciences, but surely motive is the very essence of psychological explanation.

We must be careful here that we are not making a distinction between mind and matter and making the former the subject of psychology. This old idea that mind is some sort of unique substance, not amenable to the ordinary laws of science, is one which is rightly rejected by practically all modern psychologists. It would be foolish, however, to assert that all phenomena which originally gave rise to this error *do not exist*. That is an ostrich-like reaction. Rather we must recognize the evidence and seek a more acceptable explanation for it. Such an explanation we seem to have in the notion of drives, widely and increasingly accepted to-day. This will be better understood when later chapters have been read. For the moment we must look at some more specific drives.

But before we go on to consider specific drives let us note three basic points about drives in general. Firstly, each drive has a more or less specific affect, i.e. 'feeling' associated with it. The 'hedonic tone' as this feeling is also called is usually quite obvious; as in the unpleasantness of strong hunger or fear and the pleasantness of sexual behaviour. This hedonic tone is frequently of a dual nature, being negative with regard to the continued activation of the drive without any appropriate satisfaction but positive with regard to the process concerned with satisfaction. So hunger can be very unpleasant but the satisfaction of the food need can be most enjoyable.

Secondly, the activation of a drive causes us to be attentive to certain stimuli which we might otherwise ignore. It leads to a specific scanning type of behaviour designed to discover those circumstances which will make possible the satisfaction of our need. We are alert when hungry to signs of food. The particular things sought will depend upon learning but the process of scanning is part of the drive mechanism.

Thirdly, the drive causes us to carry out behaviour which we have learned from experience to be likely to bring about satisfaction of the drive or to carry out more or less vaguely inspired random behaviour until we hit upon some action which leads to satisfaction.

We should add to this two further points: that there is a specific mechanism for activating the drive and for deactivating it. A drive has to function either when the corresponding need is great or when the opportunity for satisfaction is great, so that the development of extreme need can be conveniently forestalled. We need to be motivated to drink either when our bodies are very short of water or when a convenient opportunity to drink presents itself and our capacity will enable us to add to our reserve. Thus activation may be internal and due to tissue changes or may come about through the perception of environmental cues favourable to the satisfaction of the need.

Just as there must be a suitable mechanism for activating the drive, there must also be one for turning it off again. It has often been naïvely assumed that meeting the need will necessarily reduce the drive and nothing else could. But this is to lose sight of the real nature of the drive. Usually hunger disappears quickly after eating and long before the digestive process has done anything significant to redress the physiological deficit. Special mechanisms seem to be involved in reducing drive activation. It is as if the brain had signalled, 'O.K. boys, don't waste your batteries, we are on the way.'

HUNGER

We have taken hunger as a typical drive but, to be precise, we should perhaps have used the word in the plural, for there appears to be evidence of specific hungers according to the food deficiency. Thirst may be regarded as one of these specific hungers but the feeling of thirst may be associated with mineral deficiencies as well as with the simple need for water. After excessive perspiration the body becomes deficient in salt and under these conditions drinking water alone may fail to quench the thirst. One is left with a feeling of dissatisfaction which leaves one craving for other forms of drink.

The satisfaction of the varied food needs of the body in terms of specific hungers has been demonstrated by what has been called 'cafeteria feeding'. This has been tried out with rats and with babies, with very similar results. A variety of foods is made available and these are selected according to personal preference. Fifteen children under five years of age showed development in advance of normal growth rates under these conditions and the diets chosen agreed very well with the recommendations of the dieticians. One should, perhaps, beware of concluding that the choice of foods under these circumstances is associated with distinct experiences of need, as hunger differs from thirst. It may simply be that the dissatisfaction persists until the particular substance is supplied. On the other hand we do know that the satisfactions we derive from eating various foods are rather specific. We may like steak and strawberries but the pleasure of eating the one is quite distinct from the eating of the other. Too much of one will quickly dull our satisfaction in eating it but will leave us with our appetite for the other relatively little impaired.

These specific satisfactions may be related to specific hungers but research to date suggests that the relationship is not simple and clear-cut. There is some evidence, however, that in the case of at least a few dietary needs, deprivation does in some way alter the operation of the taste system. Human beings suffering from sugar deprivation as the result of insulin treatment found a thirty per cent sugar solution, which had previously been too syrupy, now to be pleasant and preferable to a five per cent solution previously preferred but which now seemed too weak. Parallel experiments with animals have given similar indications (but, of course, no subjective reports!). We may therefore conclude that there are some specific hungers requiring specific food intakes to reduce the drive and having drive satisfactions geared to the state of deficiency.

The situation is complicated, however, by the fact that when there is a reduction in the total food intake the demand for all foods seems to be increased and the differential choice is reduced. It is common experience that when we are not very hungry we are most finicky about what we will eat and the same is true of experimental subjects such as rats. Again a specific deficiency may increase hunger in general, or at least lead to more general eating. Further, in both rats and people, we may have a persistence in eating what seems to be 'liked' to the detriment of what is 'needed'.

What seems to emerge from all this research is that there is an unknown number of specific hungers which are themselves inter-related. These hungers are highly correlated (via physiological mechanisms) with dietary needs but not completely so. This accords with our more general finding that it is only on the average that need and drive go together; it is not a logical necessity but only an evolutionary one which may be subject to exceptions. For some needs there may be no specific drive at all because the need has been met incidentally as will be seen in the next section. Some dietary needs would certainly seem to lack appropriate drive mechanisms. In some areas of the world human beings appear to have suffered from a chronic iodine deficiency without manifesting anything recognizable as iodine hunger.

Here we must stress again that the meeting of a physiological need is not in itself necessarily satisfying to all. Satisfaction is a psychological quality and its association with biological needs is not a logical necessity but the outcome of biological history. Obviously individuals who found satisfaction in behaviour which was biologically harmful would tend to be eliminated from the species. Biologically useful drives like biologically useful reflexes tend to be retained by a species because individuals with these advantages are more likely to have opportunities to pass on these qualities to their offspring. On the whole, therefore, we find that those things which are satisfying to the individual are also beneficial to him physiologically, but this is true only in general and not in all specific cases. Thus the opium or alcohol addict may find great satisfaction in behaviour that is rapidly leading to his physiological destruction.

We shall be discussing learning later but we must observe here that we *learn* many of our likes and dislikes. Some races will eat raw grubs which would be extremely repellent to most of us. Much more than flavour is involved in such a case. We are not ready to discuss these further factors in this chapter.

THE NEED FOR AIR

Our need for food is one of which we are frequently aware because the body is frequently in a state of deficiency. The associated drive is periodically stimulated by this deficiency and its subjective aspects (the feeling of hunger) are well known to most of us, but the corresponding need for air is one of which we are only occasionally subjectively aware. That there is a strong drive associated with this, however, is easily demonstrated by depriving oneself of air for a short time. The consequent distress stimulates a violent response.

There is one very interesting point about this need for air. One tends to interpret it as a need for oxygen but, in fact, the need for oxygen is one which has no associated drive. A person may be deprived of oxygen without his feeling the deprivation subjectively at all. In fact one of the chief dangers which the aviator has to face in flying at high altitudes where the supply of oxygen is considerably reduced is that of failing to realize his need for supplementary oxygen before his physical ability is reduced too far for him to carry out the appropriate actions.

Similarly, the person who is exposed to coal gas has the chemical system whereby oxygen is circulated through the blood to the various parts of the body put out of action so that death by asphyxiation is quickly induced. The result is precisely the same as when the air supply is cut off by choking, but, whereas this latter situation is intensely distressing, the former causes no discomfort and the victim may be asphyxiated without ever appreciating his plight. The drive, then, is not associated with oxygen deficiency but with carbon dioxide excess. It is the undue concentration of carbon dioxide in the blood which is so distressing and air is required just as a medium to remove this. One could hardly ask for a neater illustration of the logical distinction between a physiological need and a psychological drive.

OTHER PHYSIOLOGICAL NEEDS

The air need we have seen to be essentially a need for elimination of one of the body's waste products. There are several related needs whose relief may cause considerable distress. Excretion and urination are the two most obvious of these. At first thought it would seem that these are not of great importance psychologically since there should be little to interfere with their satisfaction. It will be seen later, however, that these two needs may indirectly be of very great importance in the moulding of our personalities because of the training required to bring them under control in a socially approved manner, and because of the complication which may ensue in the process of training. This will be taken up in another chapter.

Another elimination need is that associated with fatigue. Fatigue products are constantly accumulating in the body and both rest and sleep are required to permit their proper elimination. Rest permits a temporary amelioration of the position but only sleep will permit a thorough spring-cleaning. The urge to rest or sleep under the stress of this need is well known, but here again we have to combat a common misunderstanding. Sleep is not a necessary result of excessive fatigue. In fact it may be very difficult to sleep in certain stages of fatigue. We have 'gone past' our sleep, as it is often expressed. Sleep is a positive response of the body which it is not always capable of making. Tiredness and fatigue are not by any means synonymous. We may feel tired and sleepy without being unduly fatigued and we may be excessively fatigued without being in any way sleepy.

In general terms we may say that sleep is the body's attempt to avoid undue fatigue. It is a protective system which comes into operation as may be most opportune. Increase of fatigue will, other things being equal, increase our tendency to sleep. The other things which must be equal are largely summed up as immediate demands for action. If the need for action is strong (as may happen with the stimulation of a major drive) there will be little tendency to sleep despite considerable fatigue. But note that the need for action cannot be just an intellectually understood one. We may *know* that keeping awake is a matter of life and death but, unless this stimulates the psychological drive system, we may still drift off to sleep, as more than one sentry has found. On the other hand, in a monotonous and unexciting environment where none of our drives are appreciably excited (say a hot Sunday morning during a boring sermon in church), we may drift off to sleep although not appreciably fatigued. It is almost as though nature were saying, 'Nothing much doing now, let's close down and prepare for future demands.' An appreciation of this distinction between the physiological fatigue system and the sleep mechanism is highly important to a proper understanding of the fatigue problem in industry and elsewhere.

Frequently mention is made of 'mental fatigue'. It is very doubtful whether this involves anything different from physical fatigue except that the sleep component may be greater. Much of the fatigue of mental work may be due to the tenseness of muscles during thinking and so obviously as physical in origin as fatigue due to running. On the other hand much mental fatigue occurs before any great demands have been made and is largely a sleepiness response to boredom. Really interesting mental work can be carried on for long periods without sign of fatigue. This question of boredom and its effects is one which we cannot discuss further at this stage.

We must finally refer to a need which is the antithesis of that for rest. It would appear that in the healthy unfatigued organism there is a positive drive towards exercise. It is difficult to envisage in what way this may be a physiological need but it does seem to manifest itself as a psychological need. This is particularly true of children and appears to motivate much of their play. Possibly fatigue, sleep, and the need for exercise, are just three aspects of a common system. There is much study to be done in this area yet. The finding of nerve centres which are associated with the control of sleeping and waking has stimulated interest, and some recent experiments with perception (see Chapter 11) have aroused further interest.

4

SPECIES NEEDS

IN the previous chapter we have discussed individual needs and related drives. We have now to consider drives which serve needs not important to the individual as such but essential for the continuation of the species. Evolutionary processes have selected those organisms which have such a physiological nature that they will engage in activities which promote the perpetuation of the race. Thus an organism so constituted that it will experience unpleasant affect if denied, and very pleasant affect if permitted to achieve, sexual intercourse will behave as if a grave individual need were at stake despite the fact that deprivement of this satisfaction will still permit his attaining a ripe old age while deprivement of his water need will lead to death in a few days.

It is convenient to consider these drives relating to the species needs in a separate class but it should be remembered that as drives they are not different from the ones talked about in the previous chapter. Psychologically what we are concerned with is not the gravity of the need with respect to the individual but the strength of the drive which only corresponds in general with the gravity of need. It will be remembered that biologically it is the species rather than the individual which is the unit concerned in evolution. Unless the species goes on there can be no individuals and so species drives could quite conceivably be greater than those relating to individual needs.

THE SEX DRIVE

Sexual needs are a very obvious example of the evolutionary selective process to which we have referred. The whole sex mechanism has meaning only in terms of species survival. The satisfaction of the sex needs is certainly not essential to individual survival in the way that the satisfaction of his food needs is. But sexual behaviour is essential to racial survival and unless members of a species show an adequate tendency to sex behaviour, the species will soon disappear. We thus find that in all existing species there is a strong sex drive and this is one of the prime sources of human motivation. The popularization of Freud's work has led to a general appreciation of this, probably to an over-emphasis, since Freud, as a psychiatrist, was dealing with maladjusted people, and the sex drive, because of social taboos, is the drive most likely to be denied normal satisfaction and so lead to adjustment difficulties.

We should at once make clear the distinction between the sex drive and what is usually referred to as love, that is romantic love. There is an intense affective aspect of sexual activity which McDougall referred to as lust and for which, provided one avoids the moral associations of the word, there appears to be no better designation. Lust without love is morally disapproved but lust is also a component of normal healthy romantic love. The other chief component comes from the parental drive. The tender protective attitude of the lover derives from this source and provides a basis for a lasting relationship instead of a transient sexual satisfaction.

It is at adolescence that the sex drive appears in full strength but Freud pointed out that it may be very important long before this. Even the infant may derive some sexual satisfaction. Not only the genitals (sex organs of either sex) but also several other skin areas, such as the mouth and the breast, are capable of giving rise to pleasurable sensations which are part of the pattern of sexual satisfaction, and may play an important part in behaviour long before adolescence. The later direction of lust may depend very much on what happens with regard to these early satisfactions, but we must defer discussion of this until we have dealt with the topic of learning.

In animals sex drive is obviously linked to gland secretion, particularly in the case of the female who manifests sexual activity at more or less regular periods when not pregnant. There is some evidence for an analogous periodicity in human females but other factors may be so important as to mask this. In particular it is to be noted that in humans sex desire continues after the menopause. Similarly with men, sex behaviour frequently continues after castration although possibly at a decreasing level. Castration before puberty, however, is quite a different story. Here again we are faced with problems of learning.

THE PARENTAL DRIVE

This undoubtedly owes its intensity to the same fact as the sex drive: its vital role in the continuation of the species. Many people have been at great pains to deny that there is any maternal (let alone paternal) instinct in human beings and have pointed out that human mothers have to be taught how to care for their babies. This is certainly a telling argument against instinctive patterns of behaviour, but, of course, a drive does not assume inherited behaviour patterns. It assumes a source of motivation which will lead to the development of appropriate behaviour, and this we certainly find in parents. By the nature of the situation psychologists have been able to do little which would demonstrate the existence of a basic parental drive, but research, such as that of Levy which demonstrated a considerable relationship between expressions of maternal feeling and endocrine activity, strongly suggests that in women at least there is a physiological basis for maternal interests. It seems likely too that men, although to a lesser degree, are influenced by the same drive.

Studies have been carried out with animals, particularly with rats, which are so convenient for such experiments, to determine the relative strength of various drives. One way of doing this is to measure the degree of punishment which an animal will accept in satisfying the drive concerned. This can be neatly measured in terms of crossing an electrified grid. In such studies the maternal drive has proved stronger than the sex, hunger, or thirst drives. Most people would be inclined to argue that human mothers are willing to make greater sacrifices for their children than are animals but this cannot be put to the test in controlled experiments. Records of some individual cases would certainly lend support.

In animals there is good evidence of an endocrine basis for their mothering activities. The injection of *prolactin* into a hen will quickly induce broodiness and virgin female rats when injected with the same hormone will mother baby rats although their previous attitude towards them was distinctly aggressive. Such startling results are not obtained with human beings. The prolactin level may be related to individual differences in the intensity of the parental drive but no one has yet demonstrated this empirically.

An interesting theory is that prolactin, which is secreted in considerable amounts throughout the lactation period, stimulates the tenderness of the mother and leads to her feeling the need for an appropriate object to mother. This maternal behaviour becomes channelled towards her own baby and leads to the rapid development of a strong attachment. The process would certainly be applicable to many animals and might be the complement of the process of imprinting which has been described by ethologists. The mallard duck will follow any moving object which is presented to it within forty hours of birth. Another bird, an animal, a man, or a mechanical contrivance will do. Once the attachment has been formed the duck will continue to follow the mother substitute, but if no moving object is presented during the first two days it will never manifest such behaviour. There appears to be some sensitization which makes it receptive to the developing of such a behaviour pattern.

The attachment of the mother to her offspring may be governed by similar principles. A duck will mother chicks, a dog will rear kittens and a cow will suckle a foal, provided they are presented appropriately. A cow will accept another calf if she is coerced into feeding it a number of times. If a substitute calf is produced before she sees her own she will accept it at once. A case has been recorded of a heifer which gave birth to a stillborn calf and accepted a boy in its place and guarded him just as jealously as a calf. If a dog approached the boy it would promptly be attacked by the heifer. If anyone else attempted to milk her only about half the usual supply would be forthcoming. Seemingly the maternal drive was activated by the secretion of prolactin and became channelled on the most likely object.

If this situation obtains, in some degree, with the human mother we can see some reason for a stronger attachment of the mother to the baby during the early years, or at least months, than of the father. It is probably wrong, however, to conclude that tenderness is manifested only during the period of abnormal prolactin secretion. Some prolactin is probably being secreted by the mother when she is not breast-feeding the baby and father, too, will have his basic rate of secretion so that hormonal influence may be operative in determining individual differences in tenderness right throughout life. It is worthy of note that helplessness and fragility will provoke the protective response in most people. A kitten, a chick, or even a delicate flower will evoke this attitude, and this may be an important component in many forms of aesthetic appreciation.

5

DRIVES AND PSYCHOLOGICAL NEEDS

THE two previous chapters have been concerned with physiological and biological drives and needs. There are other drives and needs which call for separate treatment, for example 'psychological' drives and 'emergency' drives. The former are the subject of the present chapter, the latter the subject of Chapter 6.

In calling needs 'psychological' it is not implied that they are less dependent of physiological mechanisms. Their distinctive character is that they are directed to obtaining certain experiences. This character will become clearer through the examples selected.

THE SECURITY AND AFFECTION NEED

It has been explained that the urge to 'mother' children has been established strongly in the race because of its contribution to race survival. Corresponding to this drive we appear to have a corresponding urge in children to *seek* parental attention. This behaviour in children cannot be explained in terms of learning because we find that meeting all the physical needs of children leaves them unsatisfied if parental love or a substitute is not supplied. How important this loving attention of parents is to young children is well brought out by the following extract:

The high institutional mortality of infants was discussed at the annual meeting of the American Pediatric Society in 1915. Dr Henry Chapin reported on ten infant asylums located in different cities of the United States. In all but one institution every infant under two years of age died. Hamil of Philadelphia, in discussing Chapin's paper, said ironically: 'I had the honour to be connected wth an institution in this city in which the mortality among all infants under one year of age, when admitted to the institution and retained there for any length of time, was 100 per cent. That is, no infant admitted under one year of age lived to be two years old.' Southward, speaking for conditions in New York City, said: 'I can give an instance from an institution that no longer exists in which, on account of the very considerable mortality among the infants admitted, it was customary to enter the condition of every infant on the admission card as hopeless. That covered all subsequent happenings.' Knox described a study which he had made in Baltimore. He followed 200 infants admitted to various institutions in the city. Of these almost ninety per cent died within a year. The ten per cent that lived, he said, did so, apparently, because for some reason or other the babies were taken from the institution for short times and given into the care of foster parents or relatives.*

The newborn organism must come to terms with its environment. For primitive creatures the instinct equipment is adequate to enable them to cope with environment almost at once. The baby fish can usually look after itself at once. The little chick can scratch and peck at its food almost at once but requires some parental care. The human infant is completely dependent upon its parents. This is the price we must pay for plasticity of a complicated nervous system. It is because the human being has so few fixed behaviour patterns that he is able to develop patterns adequate to complex and changing conditions. The longer the infancy period the more efficient can be the equipment of the adult. But a long infancy means that there must be adequate care always for the developing infant. This is why the urge to cherish and protect children has to be so strong in humans and,

* Harry Bakwin, 'Emotional Deprivation in Infants', *Journal of Pediatrics*, October 1949, pp. 512–21.

perhaps correspondingly, why the child seeks affectionate protection at first rather than independent coping with his world.

Much light has been thrown on the nature of this drive by some very interesting experiments recently carried out by Harlow at the University of Wisconsin. He used monkeys for his experiments since these are most closely related to the human species. He was concerned to discover whether the attachment of young monkeys to their mother was the result of her function in supplying an appropriate source of food, whether mother-love was in fact nothing more than cupboard-love.

Harlow prepared two kinds of mother substitutes. The first was constructed of wood, covered with sponge rubber, and sheathed in tan cotton terry cloth. Such a mother was warm and tender, had infinite patience, never scolded and was available twenty-four hours a day. Harlow thought they had done an excellent job in preparing this mother-substitute but was not so sure that the father monkeys held the same opinion! The second type was constructed of wire and lacked all the soft cuddly properties of the first. Nevertheless, some of the wire mother substitutes were equipped with a very important maternal attribute. They had nipples from which the baby monkeys could be supplied adequately with milk.

For four baby monkeys the wire mother was the source of food and the cloth mother not, and for another four the reverse arrangement was tried so that adequate comparisons could be made. The results were quite definite. Whether the source of milk or not, it was the cloth mothers which were sought by the babies. Apart from the actual feeding time their interest was in being cuddled rather than being near the food supply. They became attached to the cloth mothers and responded to them as to real mothers. When presented with a fear stimulus in the form of a moving toy bear eighty per cent of them sought protection from the cloth mother.

Most significant was the behaviour of the baby monkeys when placed in a strange situation with and without the cloth mother. In the former case they would clutch the cloth mother, rub their bodies against her, and seek the comfort of close contact with her. After a while they would venture from her to explore all the unusual objects in the environment but only between retreats to her protection. With her as a base of operations they plucked up sufficient courage to deal with the novel and frightening stimuli.

The situation was very different without the cloth mother. Now there were obvious signs of emotion. Frequently they would just freeze in a crouched position. Sometimes there was vocalization, rocking, or sucking. Some would run to the place where the cloth mother had previously been placed and then run from object to object, screaming and crying. The presence of the wire mother did not help and the attitude to the cloth mother was the same whether she had been the source of lactation or not. Four monkeys which had been cared for by a real monkey mother were tried out for comparison and these behaved towards her in just the same way as the experimental monkeys had done towards the cloth mother.

The important point we have to notice about these experiments is that the baby monkeys have a drive which is satisfied only by soft cuddling contact. They are motivated to seek the typical mothering behaviour which is usually lavished on children. This is the complement to the parental drive. Parents are motivated to caress, infants to seek such caresses. Again this fits into a biological evolutionary pattern. Just as baby chicks must learn to follow their mother so baby monkeys must become attached to their mothers. Notice also that the responsiveness of the baby animals does much to increase the mother's response.

THE EXPLORATORY DRIVE

This is peculiarly psychological though not unrelated to species needs. Obviously knowing and understanding may play a very significant part in survival, and it might be argued, indeed has been argued, that early experience would teach a creature to carry out exploratory behaviour, but psychologists are becoming increasingly sceptical of such an explanation. Curiosity is manifested at such an early age and by such a vast range of creatures that there seems no doubt that this is a form of behaviour which has become embedded in our drive system through its contribution to race survival.

The acceptance of such a tendency as a basic drive is crucial to the concept of psychological as opposed to purely physiological drives. Here is behaviour which is mediated by no need for any kind of physical intake nor, so far as we can discover, by any chemical tension of the body. The stimulus of something strange appears to act as a challenge. The cat or dog placed in a new room will sniff all around, examining the new environment. A rat will explore a maze without any food goal being offered. It wants to *know*. Even when a rat is put into a maze with food as a goal something more than the hunger drive seems to be operating. This is a common learning experiment used by psychologists. The rat is repeatedly asked to find its way through the maze to the food object and the way in which it learns the route is studied. In time the rat can run unerringly to the food, but, even after it has reached this stage of proficiency and while still hungry, it will occasionally wander off into strange pathways. It is curious to know something more of the maze.

The building up of knowledge under the urge of curiosity vastly increases the efficiency of an organism to cope with its environment. It becomes aware of means of need

57

satisfaction of which it would otherwise remain oblivious, learns where danger lies and how to make an effective escape from danger when threatened. It knows all the possible escape routes and the points from which threat may come. In man the same urge leads to tools, machinery, the control of natural forces, and all the facilities of civilization.

Primitive creatures may live their lives almost wholly in terms of simple response patterns which they have inherited. The higher animals have quite inadequate equipment to meet their needs in this way. Rather they begin at birth to build up a repertoire appropriate to their specific environment. This consists partly of basic skills, but in the better endowed creatures and especially in man, it consists largely in building up an appropriate background of knowledge, and it is this process which is served by the exploratory drive. Knowledge means power to control. Deficiency of knowledge is a threat and we shall see later that it may result in intense fear. Curiosity is thus one aspect of our need to master the environment.

Most of us have at some time experienced the profound satisfaction which results from the gratification of curiosity. When we have puzzled over something for a long time and have finally succeeded in understanding it we have a feeling of elation. The exploration of caves has recently become very popular with many people for whom it doubtless provides many of the thrills of primitive exploration. With its added spice of danger it doubtless satisfies a very primitive urge.

AESTHETIC AND SENSORY DRIVES

Most of the drives which we have so far considered have been associated with considerable activity. The exception has been the affection need in children, which we saw to lack any very obvious activity except perhaps crying. It should be noted that the essential feature in a drive is the affective experience in terms of which activity is continued or terminated. We go on eating while the experience is pleasurable, but as soon as it becomes distasteful we cease. Activity is undertaken to increase the affective satisfaction. In some cases, however, little activity is required to promote satisfaction and enjoyment can be relatively passive. This is true of most of the aesthetic satisfactions. We feast our eyes on a sunset but little activity is called for. Nevertheless the pursuit of such satisfaction may indirectly motivate much behaviour, e.g. an overseas trip to view objects of art.

All of our senses seem to involve affective aspects. Some sounds are displeasing, some pleasing. The same is true of colours. Man's smell equipment is poor in comparison with that of many animals, but we certainly find some odours enjoyable and others quite repulsive. Many people find the touch of velvet attractive and some find other substances disagreeable. All these affects play their part in motivating behaviour. Aesthetic enjoyment certainly involves much more than this but these sensory affects are certainly part of it.

New light has been thrown on instinctive drives from ethological studies. Ethology is the term now commonly applied to the study of animal behaviour, especially when this is in a natural setting. It was developed not by psychologists but by zoologists interested in the habits of the creatures they were studying and it is therefore the more interesting in the confirmation it brings of several psychological concepts and the new angles it suggests.

A very important observation is that many drives and behaviour patterns are activated by innate releaser mechanisms. The mating response of the male stickleback is elicited by a shape resembling a pregnant female and, provided this shape is present, the mating response follows although the object of this shape does not in other respects remotely resemble a fish. Similarly the aggressive behaviour of the male robin is produced whenever he is stimulated by a bunch of red feathers or their equivalent while he is in his own territory. Jackdaws will attack a person carrying a black cloth which represents essential aspects of a jackdaw but will be quite unconcerned if a young naked jackdaw is carried.

The Siamese fighting-fish makes a bubble nest on the surface of the water and then searches for an appropriate female to entice underneath. Love-making takes a well defined form. The male shows off his splendour by placing himself in a position which puts him broadside to his bride. She, however, must always remain facing him. If she should turn sideways his love will immediately be changed to anger and he will attack her savagely. Two releaser patterns appear to be involved. One is presented by the pregnant female and the other by a marauding male who must be fought. Perception of one of these patterns results in appropriate drive stimulation. It is possible that human beings may also have innate releaser for some of their drives. Monkeys would appear to have an instinctive fear of snakes but available evidence suggests this is not true for children. A loud noise, however, stimulates fear and may do so in a similar way.

Harlow's work, described in our last chapter, should be considered in this connexion. The sensation of cuddly contact evidently is related to the process of child–mother attachment. Since the offspring of the higher animals depend so much upon parental care for their early welfare it is important that they should maintain close contact with parent or parents. The psychological need for caressing serves this purpose and is the reciprocal of the parental drive towards caressing. Human mothers find much satisfaction in cuddling their babies and it is appropriate that the babies should appreciate it. This is the basis of the love bond which develops in human and many animal families.

Possibly other mechanisms serve these reciprocal love-protection drives. Bowlby has suggested that smiling may be one of these. The work of Spitz strongly suggests that the baby's smile is evoked by an innate releaser pattern (although he does not himself suggest this explanation) and there can be little doubt that the mother's affection is reinforced by the smiling response. Spitz and Wolf demonstrated that the smile stimulus must include the shape of a human face (front view) with two eyes and that there must be motion, such as nodding. Provided these requirements were met by a mask or a dummy, babies of different races and with different backgrounds of experience would smile.

The implications of this are intriguing. Many people have wondered at some time why human beings smile. It obviously serves no direct physical need. But if it is part of the system serving the racial need for effective reproduction it makes good sense. Furthermore we get some insight into the social implications of smiling in adult life. The smile of the adult is by no means restricted to expression of amusement. It is more than anything an indication of good will and we use it to indicate our favourable attitude towards people.

6

THE EMERGENCY DRIVES

PREVIOUS chapters have described drives concerned with the individual needs of the organisms, with the species needs, and with the distinctively psychologious needs. We shall consider next drives of a more general kind, related not so much to specific needs as to the attainment of a broad adjustment of the individual to his environment. Two of these we shall describe as 'emergency' drives because they are concerned to mobilize the energies of the individual to cope with an emergency situation. These two drives of fear and anger are closely related to a further drive which has been proposed under the title of 'excitement' because they all come under the general description of what is called *emotion*. The fourth drive which we shall consider here is linked to fear as also serving the general aim of security attainment although in a much less spectacular way.

THE EMERGENCY SYSTEM

When people become particularly intense in their behaviour we describe them as being emotional. Considerable research has been done on the nature of emotion. It has been found that, not only is strong affect present, but that there are many physiological changes involved. The importance of these physiological elements is so great that James and Lange (independently) put forward a theory of emotion which made the physiological changes primary. As James puts it, 'we feel sorry because we cry, angry because we strike, afraid because we tremble' rather than the reverse. 'Without the bodily states following on the perception the latter would be purely cognitive in form, pale, colourless, destitute of emotional warmth.' This was a startling theory in the days when mind was usually thought of as something which could operate independently of the body and it motivated a considerable amount of research. In particular, people who have nerve injuries which prevent their feeling the physiological changes have been studied to see whether they still experience normal emotions. Such patients report that they do experience emotion and this has cast considerable doubt on the James–Lange theory. It has also been argued that the experience of fear is frequently too rapid to allow for the indirect route suggested by James. This and other evidence has led to the rejection of the theory, but most psychologists would agree that it was right in emphasizing the importance of the physiological aspects of emotion.

A hypothalamic theory of emotion is widely accepted to-day. The hypothalamus is a small portion of the brain in the middle of the head at about the level of the eyes. It is the centre which appears to add emotional intensity to our experiences. People vary very much in the degree to which they make emotional responses and in some cases the emotion can be quite incapacitating. Some patients suffer from a severe chronic anxiety which magnifies all their worries and makes life a burden to them. In extreme cases a brain operation is performed on such patients whereby some of the brain fibres are cut in the vicinity of the thalamus. The result is usually a miraculous reduction in anxiety. Worries which were thought grave enough to demand suicide may now seem of little importance. One explanation for such a change is that the nerve currents are hindered from flowing through the thalamus and so to the hypothalamus.

There are two major emotional responses, which may be described as emergency drives. These are *fear* and *anger*. It used to be claimed that the physiological concomitants of these two responses were identical but recent evidence gives cause to doubt this. That common elements are involved is certain, but it is also certain that some of these elements enter also into other responses which could not be described as involving either fear or anger. It would appear that the emotional system comes into operation as a booster when special demands are likely to be made on the body. In so operating it takes three main forms and we shall now consider each of these in turn.

FEAR

One of the chief occasions for emergency response is when danger threatens. We then experience the well known fear response. This is accompanied by trembling of the limbs, goose-flesh, paling of the skin, enlargement of the pupils of the eyes, quickened pulse, deeper breathing, and an interference with the digestive system which is popularly described as 'my stomach turned over'. The digestive disturbance extends to the salivary glands, which refuse to function and so lead to a dry mouth. In ancient times the Chinese are said to have made use of this latter fact to establish the guilt of a prisoner. The suspect was asked to chew rice and later spit it out. If the rice was still dry his guilt was held to be established. What happened, of course, was that the guilty person was so frightened that he could not salivate. Provided the innocent person did not panic he was safe, but obviously the procedure was likely to break down except in a community where there was high confidence in this method of trial, so that the innocent person felt quite certain that he would be all right.

But fear is not just this conglomeration of physiological symptoms. It involves also a typical form of affect which cannot be described but which all of us probably know in some degree from our own experience. It is often accompanied by a feeling of impotence and almost of paralysis, a tendency to shrink away from danger. This may give way later to the wild panic of flight.

We have given as the cause for all this the perception of danger but we must now enlarge upon this. We have to notice that this fear behaviour often occurs when there is no actual danger at all and even *when the person involved knows there is no danger*. A harmless snake or even a harmless insect may provoke paroxysms of fear and no amount of demonstration of the lack of danger will abate it at all. This is a good example of how a drive operates. Reason is the servant of drives and not their master. Reason can control a drive only by invoking another powerful drive to combat it. But this question of control is one which we must consider later. Here our concern is with the drive stimulus. In some cases there appears to be an innate connexion between a certain stimulus situation and the arousal of a drive. In the case of fear at least two situations appear to be innately attached to it as stimuli. A loud noise or a sudden withdrawal of support will arouse fear in most infants. It has been denied that children have an instinctive fear of snakes but it seems to be established that monkeys have and this tends to make one question the reliability of the experiment carried out with children. The difficulties of this type of research will be better understood when we have discussed the concept of conditioning in the next chapter.

The level at which fear operates may be brought out well by an illustration. If a tiger were at large in a big city like London and selected a new victim every day you can imagine with what trepidation people would venture forth into the streets. The menace of modern traffic, however, is much greater than this, and yet Londoners go about their business usually quite oblivious of the danger which they run.

ANGER

Some of the physiological concomitants of anger are the direct reverse of those of fear. Thus, instead of a dry mouth, we tend to the opposite so that the expression, 'foaming at the mouth' has been used to describe this condition. Instead of a pallor we tend to become flushed with anger. Note the expression 'purple with anger'. There is no goose-flesh or tendency for the hair to stand on end. The eyes, instead of being enlarged, tend to be narrowed with the brows contracted over them. Trembling and tendency to paralysis is replaced by a firm tensing of the muscles. The shrinking feeling typical of fear is replaced by the opposite. We feel as though we shall explode if we can't let off steam in some way. Pulse rate quickens as in fear but the pulse strength probably increases more. Likewise the depth of breathing probably increases more than in fear.* The differences in breathing and heart beat, however, are much more open to doubt than in the case of other symptoms and may depend upon the violence of the response more than upon the drive involved.

All the physiological effects we have described above, as also those described in connexion with fear, are controlled by a network of nerves called the *autonomic system*, supplemented by the effect of hormones discharged into the blood stream. This system is concerned with internal body regulation. It is our Department of Internal Affairs. Bodily adjustments required to meet changes in the environment, more particularly sudden changes, are mediated through its control. Sudden changes of temperature stimulate a typical pattern of physiological response. In the case of cold we have trembling of the limbs (shivering), goose-flesh, paling

---

* The breathing change in fear may be related to the need for concentrated attention which may require the noise of breathing to be suspended for short periods.

of the skin, quickened pulse, deeper breathing. All these, it will be noted, are also concomitants of fear. Correspondingly, the responses to heat parallel those of anger, e.g. sweating and flushing. It is interesting to note how this is reflected in common language. We become 'heated' in a violent argument, get 'hot under the collar', 'boil with rage', 'get steamed up', 'let off steam'. On the other hand we have expressions like 'frozen with fear', 'my blood ran cold', 'a cold sweat', 'a cold shiver down my spine', and countless others.

The stimulus to anger is some kind of frustration. One absent-mindedly brushes a fly away. It returns and one makes another effort. After a few unsuccessful efforts our ire rises and we determine to do something effective. It is interesting to observe, however, that what takes place is not merely a strengthening of our resolve. There is always something personal about it. We wish to hurt, to punish the frustrating agent, and even an inanimate object may become the object of vicious blows. The watch we fail to repair may be smashed up. We may kick a door, snap off an offending twig. The typical reaction is, 'I'll teach you!' Obviously such a reaction has had considerable importance in racial history in so far as it has enabled us to cope with the opposition of other creatures. We have been motivated to fight for our rights or, at least, for our needs. For this purpose the energies of the body have been mobilized to provide muscular capacity beyond the ordinary. In anger we become capable of feats of strength beyond our normal capacity. The same is true of fear when activity ensues. It is related that a man chased by a bull jumped over a wall which he was unable to climb back over when the danger was averted.

On the other hand it should be noted that, although muscular strength is increased by anger, behaviour which requires careful reasoning may be very much hindered. As life becomes more dependent on intelligence, violent anger becomes less and less appropriate and in the age of atom bombs uncontrolled anger may be the prelude to race suicide.

The autonomic nervous system is usually considered as having two main divisions – the sympathetic and the parasympathetic – which tend to be antagonistic in function, but the fear–cold, anger–heat contrast does not coincide with this division. It has been suggested that these patterns are related rather to the contrast between nerves which function by the action of an adrenaline-like chemical and those which function through acetylcholine. Other investigators have suggested another contrast in terms of two forms of adrenaline. More research will be required before we are at all certain of the physiology of the autonomic nervous system, but the reader should be warned that the classical descriptions quoted in many textbooks probably require considerable amendment, particularly with regard to their ascription of a common sympathetic response pattern to both fear and anger. Much confusion seems to have been caused here because the cold–heat systems function as a balance and, when pushed in one direction, do not simply return to equilibrium, but swing well to the opposite side before settling down to rest. Thus cold first produces pallor, but after a time a reaction sets in and the skin becomes flushed. The pallor is due to constriction of the fine blood vessels in the skin and the result is to prevent the blood from circulating to the surface of the body in the normal way. This conserves heat in the more vital part of the body. It is a useful short-term response. If the body has adequate reserves, however, it takes more drastic action and builds up a higher level of metabolism ('burning' of food reserves). The supply of heat is thus increased and the heat side of the system takes over with consequent flushing.

Similar antithetical reactions can be observed with regard

to fear. The pallor so typical of fear ('as white as a sheet') gives way to flushing on recovery. People observing fear responses thus often report flushing as a symptom and so find that it involves the same symptoms as anger. Again, a primary anger stimulus may give way to a secondary cold type of response. The degree to which the secondary response occurs depends on a number of factors, but a major factor appears to be the ability of the organism to cope with the situation. In the case of fear the subject may be able to withdraw from the situation. In successful flight the primary response soon disappears (as, in successfully coping with cold, the initial pallor, shivering, etc., gives way to flushing). Where no adequate measures can be taken against fear, however, its primary inhibitory effects appear to be accentuated and the violence of flight is replaced by a passive inertia and an exaggerated insensitivity to pain. Livingstone, the African explorer, who was seized by a lion and later rescued, remarks on the detachment with which he was able to view the situation. A friend of the writer who was apparently drowned but revived by artificial respiration, related a similar attitude to the calamity. She had accepted the situation with a fatalism which was far from her normal attitude to life. Numerous accounts of soldiers in terrifying situations have shown that, although they may have experienced highly disturbing pangs of fear in anticipating the experience or in recalling it later, they were relatively indifferent to the danger during the critical time. This is not just the reaction of the abnormally brave man. The writer has no pretensions to bravery but has twice been threatened with extreme danger and has been astounded by his fatalistic reaction to it.

There is an important practical application to this finding with regard to fear situations. It is worth bearing in mind that the most feared events never happen, that is, they never happen in the psychological sense. Because small threats or distant threats produce considerable distress we naturally assume that, with increased threat, our distress will be correspondingly magnified. It is this expectation which is untrue. Large doses of fear become stupefying rather than terrifying.

Another practical application in this area is worth commenting on. We have already noted that it is the lesser forms of fear which are most upsetting. Extreme fear brings its own relief, sometimes even fainting and oblivion, but a continuing fear stimulus of lower intensity can be extremely distressing if it is not possible to take appropriate action. When it is possible to be physically active in dealing with the situation, however, the situation may become thrilling rather than frightening. This was well illustrated in bombing raids during the Second World War. Ordinary citizens were called upon to take shelter and wait passively until the raid was over. Civil Defence personnel were required to go out to rescue wounded and trapped and so were usually exposed to greater danger than the ordinary citizen, and yet they were much less affected by fear. It is related that during the sinking of a ship one passenger panicked badly and became a menace to the orderly evacuation of the ship. An understanding officer appealed to him for help, gave him a rope, and told him to 'pull like hell'. The passenger pulled, and the impression that he was now doing something helpful quietened his nerves. The fact that the rope was simply attached to one of the deck fixtures in no way lessened the usefulness of his effort!

EXCITEMENT

To the two major emotions of fear and anger it has been suggested that we should add a third. Excitement certainly involves the autonomic system, but it need not partake of either fear or anger. Both of these responses seem to be basically unpleasant, but excitement may be highly pleasurable. There is a common element, however, in the functioning of the autonomic system. In both anger and fear there is some preparation of the body for violent activity. The digestive system is inhibited so that energy which would normally be used in this direction can now be mobilized for fight or flight when necessary. Blood pressure rises and any tendency to sleep is dissipated. It is this common element in fear and anger which seems largely to constitute excitement.

In some respects anger and fear are antithetical but the antithesis of excitement is rather sleep. It is a common experience that, when we are excited, it is very difficult for us to settle down to sleep. We might almost think of excitement as intensity of wakefulness and it is interesting to notice that it is the hypothalamus which controls the sleep function. It is this centre which invests experience with significance. As it becomes more active events seem more important to us. We attend more closely and perceive with greater clarity. Our muscles become tense and ready for strenuous activity. The blood sugar content of the blood increases and generally we begin to live more intensely.

The hypothalamus, with the linked autonomic, system may be thought of as a *feedback system*. Feedback has become a common term since the modern development of automatic control by engineers and the construction of various types of automata, but a type of feedback has long been known in the dynamo and even earlier in the steam engine. The dynamo provides a useful analogy. When the armature of a dynamo is rotated it produces a small current of electricity. Some of this is fed back through the many layers of wire surrounding the field magnets and the magnetism of these is thereby increased. The result is an increase in the production of current which strengthens the magnets still more, and so it goes on until output is at a maximum for the given speed of rotation. Without the feedback to the field magnets the output of the dynamo would be negligible. A parallel situation seems to hold for the emotional system. It magnifies the importance of events. If the hypothalamus is isolated by appropriate lesions this feedback ceases and the organism relaxes into sleep.

People differ considerably in their degree of autonomic feedback. Some, like Mr Micawber, are always up in the clouds or down in the depths. They swing from one extreme to another and every trifling event is pregnant with significance for them. Others are stolid and indifferent, never much thrilled by success and never greatly put out by failure. They are inclined to be contemptuous about their flighty, excitable neighbours. It is notorious that actors and artists are 'temperamental'. These people are able to appeal to the emotions of others because they are themselves emotionally sensitive. A good actor cannot merely imagine a given situation but can 'feel' what it would be like in such a situation. Art without feeling is dead. Technical excellence in a musician may be admired, but if his rendering lacks emotional content it is cold and lifeless. The artist must have more than an ability to draw. The pictures of some great painters are hopeless by photographic standards, but they are able to produce an emotional effect which the original would fail to excite in less sensitive mortals. But this emotional sensitivity, which is the key to their professional success, makes them difficult to work with because everything matters so profoundly to them. They tend to behave in superlatives. Like high-voltage circuits they must be handled with great care.

We have to remember that emotion adds to the zest of life whenever we are controlling things satisfactorily to our own ends. For this reason people will deliberately seek excitement. Fear-arousing situations will be sought out provided there is a good chance of mastery. Overcoming danger provides a thrill. The heightened intensity of living is distinctly pleasurable. Mild anger, too, may be stirring without being unduly unpleasant and may provide a welcome stimulant to a lethargic nervous system. Just so, substances with distasteful odour may be very pleasant if sufficiently diluted. Adrenaline, which in large doses has an inhibiting effect, acts as a stimulant when taken in small amounts. Frustration which can be overcome, dangers which can be successfully avoided, are similarly stimulating. They make demands but we can meet them. Lack of demands on the body leads to lethargy and sleep.

It must not be thought from what we have said that anger or fear is necessary to excitement. The scientist on the eve of a new discovery may be profoundly excited. The man who has just been told that he has won a large sum of money may be similarly affected. In the latter case there may be no element of fear nor of anger at all, but the money may represent the fulfilment of long cherished desires. The making of the discovery may for the scientist, too, be the fulfilment of a long cherished desire. Perhaps excitement always involves a step towards the satisfaction of important desires. Success is the prime stimulus to excitement, as is failure to its antithesis: depression. Depression is aptly named in that all bodily functions become depressed and there may be actual physical wastage. Excitement, on the other hand, involves a general heightening of all bodily processes outside the digestive group.

INTER-RELATION OF DRIVES

Now that we have completed our description of the individual drives it will be useful to consider how they function within a system. The diagram on p. 74 (Fig. 2) endeavours to do this. We can think of the person as having two primary needs: to maintain an adequate basis of security and to attain a satisfactory level of achievement in the positive satisfaction of individual and species drives. In so far as the security need is threatened there will be experience of fear and emergency action taken. This security normally has a dual basis: understanding of the nature of the environment and so the action required to operate safely and successfully within it, and the social support provided primarily by the family. For the child the latter predominates. The parent is sought primarily for 'contact' satisfactions ('cuddling'), as we have described, and then increasingly for protection. The parents' part in this process is secured through their sex and parental drives.

With increasing age the child's cognitive needs become greater and curiosity serves as a constant stimulus for it to extend its cognitive understanding. A major portion of its activities become devoted to various ways of exploring its world and developing an adequate 'cognitive reference frame', and incidentally numerous motor skills. All this is a preparation to meet its needs before they arise. Before a drive is activated and action is called for it has already equipped itself with the necessary knowledge and skills.

When the security system is threatened fear is aroused and highly motivated efforts made to cope with the situation. This is aided by the automatic development of widespread physiological changes appropriate to the crisis. Correspondingly when some obstacle obstructs the satisfac-

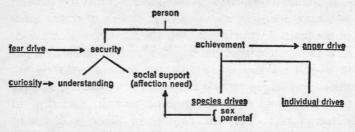

Fig. 2. The inter-relation of drives.

tion of a drive, or any highly motivated activity, anger is provoked and another pattern of physiological responses produced.

Finally it is to be noted, although not included in the diagram (Fig. 2), that whenever a stimulus occurs it will produce some degree of activation over the reticular system, and some degree of emotional excitement according to its significance for the drive system as a whole. All this will become clearer as we proceed.

DRIVES AND THE NERVOUS SYSTEM

The concept of drives has been viewed with suspicion by a number of psychologists because it is so easy to postulate an appropriate drive to explain any observed pattern of behaviour. We can justify the postulation of a drive only if we can show there is an innate source of behaviour. For the most part this can be achieved only by showing that people with very varied background experience and with little opportunity to influence one another have similar forms of motivation. So there can be little doubt about hunger, thirst, sex drive, and the like but many suggested drives may be queried. Now a new line of evidence is opening up. Where a drive can be stimulated by neurological means it would appear that we have much more certainty as to its nature. Some of this evidence we must now consider.

A number of experimenters have shown that it is possible to control eating by stimulation or cutting of certain parts of the brain. Hetherington and Ranson found that lesions in a particular part of the hypothalamus caused albino rats to overeat enormously so that they became extremely fat. Miller and others at Yale found that by electrical stimulation they could make a rat drink at will. Similarly the effects of pain, fear, and rage could all be produced by suitable electrical stimulation. Sleeping or waking and sexual activity also have been found to have appropriate 'centres'.

Olds and Milner found that electrical stimulation in the septal region of the rat's brain had rewarding effects similar to drive satisfaction. The evidence strongly suggests that something in the nature of a very pleasant affective experience was being produced in the rats. The implication is that affect is the result of stimulation of appropriate areas of the brain. If so we may have evidence for a neurological correlate of affective experience. This will certainly make the concept more appealing to some psychologists and will open the way to direct physical control of psychological mechanisms. Some of the possibilities are almost frightening.

Neurological research in relation to psychological principles is only in its early stages. We can expect many new discoveries during the next few years and these will doubtless help us to understand better many forms of human behaviour. A knowledge of neurology is becoming more and more important to the psychologist.

MODIFICATION OF DRIVES
AND REFLEXES

7

LEARNING

HUMAN beings live in a complex and changing environment so that it is impossible for them to be adequately equipped at birth to cope with it. Instead of a complicated set of behavioural patterns they have the means of learning the appropriate response systems. This makes for flexibility and efficiency. Even so we find old people with outmoded skills and decreased ability to learn new ones. The man who rode a horse or drove a buggy needs now to learn how to handle a motor-car and will doubtless soon need the skill to manage a plane. Ability to learn is highly important and is one of the chief features which distinguish the higher from the lower organisms. We must now study some of the principles which underlie the learning process.

Early this century the Russian physiologist Ivan Pavlov, who was carrying out research on the digestive processes, observed that dogs would salivate before food was presented to them. The signal for salivation was something which had been associated with food. He proceeded to carry out careful experiments and discovered that if he sounded a particular musical note just prior to presenting food and repeated this procedure a number of times, the dog would then salivate to the tone alone. With the aid of a special attachment he was able to measure the amount of salivation, and found that the more frequently the tone and food had been paired, the more effective the tone was in stimulating salivation, until the maximum effect was produced. In one experiment after 31 pairings a response of 65 drops of saliva was obtained. The response thus obtained is known as the conditioned response, and the new stimulus as the conditioned stimulus. The Russian word is more correctly translated as *conditional* but the traditional English form is not likely to be displaced now.

Now it is to be noted that the process of conditioning involves something deeper than an intellectual association of certain circumstances with eating. Without being conditioned human beings soon learn that the dinner bell is a signal for dinner and will respond to it by going to the dining-room. The bell may produce no salivary response and we may be quite uninterested in food at the time. The conditioned response, however, is an involuntary one and usually follows the stimulus much faster than a similar voluntary response could. In many cases a similar voluntary response is impossible. This is true of the salivary response since we cannot salivate at will. It is true of most reflexes. For example, we are normally quite unaware of the pupillary reflex which regulates the amount of light entering the eye, and we certainly cannot enlarge or decrease the size of the pupil of the eye at will. Nevertheless it has been found that appropriate pairing of a conditioned stimulus with the unconditioned light stimulus will eventually result in the conditioned stimulus becoming effective. This conditioning, however, is much more difficult to achieve than is that of the salivary gland. It is interesting to note, though, that if the conditioned stimulus chosen is one which is under the control of the subject himself, such as the sounding of a bell, he can in this way gain voluntary control over the reflex.

This is quite an important point since in this way we can gain control of all responses which are subject to conditioning. There are possibilities here which have not yet been exploited to any extent by Western peoples.

The involuntary nature of the conditioned reflex is well illustrated by a method which was developed for testing simulated deafness. A graduated sound source was used as the conditioned stimulus and an electric shock as the unconditioned stimulus. After suitable conditioning the subject would make a withdrawal response to the sound just as if the electric shock were given and so proved that he must have heard the signal. By graduating the sound stimulus it was possible to decide at just what level the sound became inaudible and so the hearing acuity of the subject could be assessed without his verbal cooperation. Similar methods have been used in experiments with animals where verbal response is impossible. Ingenious modifications of this principle enable a considerable amount of information about animal functioning to be obtained. The problem of whether animals and insects can distinguish colours is neatly solved in this way.

GENERALIZATION AND DIFFERENTIATION

Pavlov found that when a dog had been conditioned to a musical tone other tones would produce the same effect though to a lesser degree, depending on the similarity to the original tone. This effect is known as generalization. If he now continued to present the various tones but offered food only with the original tone, the dog reached a stage where it would respond only to the correct musical note and fail to salivate to the unrewarded (technically *non-reinforced*) ones. By choosing tones very close together it was possible to differentiate in terms of very fine differences depending on the ability of the animal to distinguish between one note and another. It will be noticed that in this way it was possible to assess the ability of the dog to distinguish pitch. Dogs proved capable of making distinctions in terms of a fraction of a musical interval.

INHIBITION

A further interesting discovery made by Pavlov was that when differentiation had been achieved the non-reinforced stimuli were not just ignored. The animal was still making a response but in the negative direction. He did something positive to *restrain* response. The conditioned stimulus, if presented immediately after the differentiated stimulus, proved to be ineffective. It was almost as though the dog had put on the brakes and was no longer ready to proceed. With varying time intervals between the differentiated stimulus and the conditioned stimulus there were varying degrees of response to the latter until, if sufficient time had elapsed, the conditioned stimulus produced its normal response. This phenomenon was known as *inhibition*.

Another interesting point about inhibition was that there appeared to be a space effect similar to the time effect. If instead of using musical notes as the conditioned stimuli, the experimenter used tactual contacts with various parts of the dog's body and differentiated one of these, the inhibitory effect of stimulating it appeared to pass as a wave over the whole body. The response at any of the conditioned points depended on distance from the differentiated point and the time since its stimulation. The response to a distant point thus falls to zero and then slowly builds up again.

The reader will notice that conditioning of the type studied by Pavlov consists essentially of learning new cues for behaviour, so that the appropriate response can be made sooner. The value of this is obvious with the defensive responses. If the animal threatened with an electric shock responds soon enough, it may avoid the shock completely. Generally the extension of the cue or stimulus system adds to the efficiency of the reflex. But conditioning applies to drives as well as reflexes, and here, too, it leads to their better functioning.

CONDITIONED DRIVES

Drive conditioning is well exemplified in the case of fear. In extreme cases a conditioned response can be produced by only one reinforcement. During the last war the writer was driving along a suburban road during the evening when a v2 fell a short distance ahead, completely demolishing a public house where a dance was in progress. There were a large number of wounded in addition to the poor folk who had been the victims of the direct hit, and helping to give first aid to these emphasized the danger he had avoided. Some days later he was waiting for a train connexion when a shunting engine shot upwards a shower of sparks with an effect very similar to the exploding of the v2. For a second there surged through his body a throb of unreasoning fear, certainly a conditioned response, and, strangely enough, more frightening than the original experience while it lasted.

Most of our fears are acquired in this way. For the young child rats are no more to be feared than cats, but among adults fear of the former is quite widespread. Conditioning has been at work again. The particular mode of conditioning in this case warrants special attention. The unconditioned stimulus is not noise or lack of support but the manifest fear of a human companion, usually the mother. Fear is highly contagious, more particularly from parent to child since the child looks to the parent for security, and the sight of a frightened parent suggests that there is no longer any certainty of security in that direction. Parents' fears are thus strongly reinforcing and a single occasion may be sufficient to bring about conditioning with regard to rats and mice.

All our drives are subject to conditioning in this way and

we shall see in a later chapter how this principle operates as a factor moulding the development of our personalities. We shall, therefore, not spend further time at this stage illustrating this type of conditioning. The important thing is that the reader should remember that in this way drives become linked to appropriate stimuli and so called into operation at the optimal time. The hunger drive is stimulated when appropriate forms of food are available, the sex drive when a suitable mate offers, the parental drive when mothering behaviour is demanded, and so on.

OPERANT CONDITIONING

We have now to consider another form of conditioning which differs from the Pavlovian type in that it relates not to stimulus but to response. In the former case we graft on a new stimulus (e.g. a musical note); in the latter case we graft on a new response. This kind of conditioning is especially important in the case of drives where there may be no inherited pattern of response at all.

We may take as an example some experiments which Thorndike carried out with cats. He put them in boxes from which they could escape (and so get food) by pressing appropriate levers. The situation was quite new to the cat which had no idea what to do. Stimulated by hunger it prowled restlessly about the box, pushed, scratched, bit, and generally made all the responses in its repertoire. Finally, by luck, it operated the lever and was able to emerge. On the second occasion the cat was still nonplussed but managed to do the right thing a little sooner. With repeated trials the time required for escape gradually decreased until finally the cat could carry out the appropriate response at once. This response, because always rewarded, becomes a conditioned one.

Now this type of conditioning differs from the classical

form, not merely in that it refers to change of response instead of change of stimulus, but because the pairing process is not always automatic. Any response which works will do. The animal may press the lever with its nose, paw, body, or incidentally in turning round. Whichever response occurs first is more likely to recur and so finally become conditioned. When conditioned it continues in the accepted form and irrelevant aspects are likely to be conserved. If an unnecessary turning round has become tied up with the response the animal will continue with this as part of the response. But, although the pairing is achieved by what is called 'trial and error' (perhaps it would have been better to say 'trial and success'), the basis of the linkage may not be essentially different from the classical conditioning.

This question as to whether classical and operant conditioning have different bases is one which has been responsible for a major division in the schools of learning theory. If a common basis for the two kinds of conditioning could be found, a number of problems would disappear and important grounds for disagreement be removed. The present writer has suggested that this might be done through the concept of attention. It may be argued that those mental events become bonded which share common attention. The importance of reinforcement in operant learning would then lie in its attention-producing effects.

An outstanding fact about mental experiences is their variation in degree of salience. Certain aspects become salient, the focus of attention, while others are neglected. It is interesting to note that this is not just a matter of directing attention to particular aspects of neurological patterns already present in the brain but that this process actually modifies the degree to which an impression is neurologically present at all. Hernandez-Peon, Schere, and Jovet recorded the amount of neurological activation produced in the brain of a cat when it was listening to a series of auditory clicks. During this process the cat was presented with the stimulus of two mice in a bottle. The effect was the virtual *disappearance of the neurological response to the auditory stimulus*. This is highly important since any memory effects obviously depend upon actual neurological response and, if attention controls this, we can expect it to control what is remembered. It seems very likely, therefore, that conditioning is dependent upon the various factors which direct attention so that we have a similar basis for classical and operant conditioning.

A problem arises, however, with regard to the use of the word *learning*. We talk of the cat having learned how to get out of the box. Is this learning process the finding of the successful response or the conditioning of the response or both? Unfortunately current practice is not clear about this and the word *learning* tends to be used rather loosely. To avoid confusion we may refer to the finding of the appropriate response as *problem solving* and the method by which it is here achieved as *trial and error*.

BUILDING RESPONSE PATTERNS

The difference between problem solving and the conditioning effects which bring about retention is still more confused when the response is not a simple one but involves a number of distinct steps. This is typified by the maze situation where the subject, animal or human, has to work out a serial pattern of responses. The major learning here is of a backwards type. Consider the simple cases where there are four choice points, A, B, C, and D. The correct choice at D leads immediately to the goal and is so rewarded. We tend to remember this choice while still very confused about our meanderings in the earlier part of the maze. But now when we make the correct choice at C we immediately recognize that we now know the rest of the way. The correct choice at

C is thus reinforced and we soon retain it. The way is now open for adequate reinforcement of the correct choice at B and so on. This is the chief trend in learning, but it should be noted that choices which quickly lead into disappointing blind alleys are eliminated early, wherever they may occur.

The learning of a skill is somewhat like learning a maze.

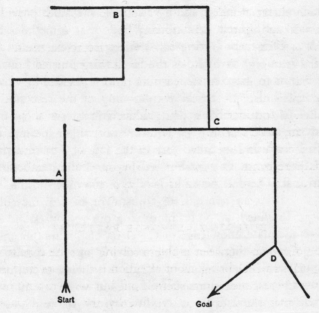

Fig. 3. Learning a maze.

Common opinion tends to stress the importance of practice. We say, 'Practice makes perfect', but this is certainly not true. In an experiment with dart throwing, subjects were given long continued practice, but each time they threw a dart the light was switched off before they could see the result. The dart was then removed from the board under cover of a screen and the throw recorded. Under these circumstances their scores deteriorated rather than improved. The value of practice is that it enables us to discover what works. It makes possible the conditioning process but unless we know the results of our effort there can be no reward and so no reinforcement.

Few people can wag their ears but most have all the necessary muscular equipment, and it is only a matter of learning. A subject who endeavours to master this skill contorts all his head and facial muscles in a variety of ways and, provided he can see himself in a mirror, finds that sometimes his efforts seem to be having some effect. He concentrates on the sort of effort which has produced this result and finally he begins to get consistent results. More practice improves the new skill.

Let us consider for a while what is involved in the improvement of a skill. First we must note that experimentation in approach is called for. In the case of dart throwing this experimentation is initiated by our failure to achieve our goal. The dart was a little high or too much to the left so we make an appropriate adjustment in our muscular effort. Provided we go on modifying our responses and receive adequate knowledge of the effect of this modification we go on learning. But if the 'feedback' of success fails, as in the peculiar conditions of the dart-throwing experiment or because all our efforts succeed alike as when we sharpen a knife, improvement ceases. In industry we find people carrying out skilled jobs with no sign of improvement over many years until given special training which may result in phenomenal improvement in a very short time. Of what does this training consist? It provides incentive for further experimentation and supplies knowledge of results. But it does this not merely in a general way but with specific direction to areas where the experience of the teacher tells him improvement is most likely. The teacher is able to take apart the complex process and enable the learner to improve each part separately. He is able to set sub-goals. He demonstrates a step and then, by telling the learner how well he is succeeding, makes possible the improvement of this unit.

We have already remarked how in operant conditioning irrelevant responses may be retained because they are associated with success as in the case of the cat turning round before pressing a lever. Human learning is full of instances where clumsy or unnecessarily complex methods are used just because they were found to work. A good example is in typewriting. The average amateur begins with one or two fingers and learns to produce passable results in this way. Yet no matter how much he practises he will never reach competition standards. A teacher will set him a new set of sub-goals which will finally greatly improve his efficiency, but which, for a time, will greatly slow up his typing ability and so would never have been conditioned in terms of his over-all achievement.

THE ROLE OF THE TEACHER

It may be useful to detail the various functions which can be carried out by the teacher in developing skills :

1. He can analyse the task into appropriate sub-units within the grasp of the learner. For example, most people find it quite impossible to learn a complex dance just by observation of the skilled performer but can cope with a short sequence of steps.

2. He can set the goal or sub-goal by demonstration. It should be noted, however, that the demonstration does set the goal rather than show the learner how to do it. Once the goal has been set repeated demonstration may be relatively useless. It is too easy for the expert to say, 'Look, this is how it is done', and then go through the action with a tantalizing facility which gives the learner no further clues at all.

No amount of demonstration of ear wagging helps us to wag our own ears. We have to experiment for ourselves.

3. He can play a vital part in indicating to the learner when he is succeeding and when failing. This is important when the learner has no simple standard of success. In learning to draw, for example, he may have a very poor idea of his success.

4. He can suggest specific improvements at any stage. 'Hold your arm higher', 'Watch your left shoulder', 'Make a longer sweep to the right'. From his intimate knowledge of the skill the teacher can in this way tremendously shorten the time required for learning. It should be realized, though, that his ability to do all this depends not so much upon his own mastery of the particular skill, but upon his knowledge of how skilled actions appear to the observer. For this reason the most highly skilled performers often fail miserably as teachers, and a person who has not himself acquired the skill at all may be an excellent teacher. A swimming coach may do very effective teaching without ever entering the water. Of course, one would not recommend the selection of unskilled persons as teachers. Some experience in the skill is highly desirable, but it should be remembered that it is the external knowledge of the skill which is most essential, and the teacher should always be chosen for his excellence in teaching and not in performance. Teaching and performance call for different abilities and it should be no reflection on a teacher that he is himself not a top-rank performer. There is much confusion about this in many quarters.

5. The teacher can help to maintain the morale of the learner during periods when he feels he is making little progress. In this connexion knowledge of the plateau phenomenon is important. Progress is seldom steadily forward. There is rapid improvement and then a period of stagnation before the upward trend is resumed. One factor in this effect

is probably the hierarchical aspect of learning. In learning to type, for example, there is rapid progress as the learner becomes familiar with the position of the various letters on the typewriter. Progress is resumed again as he begins to build up word knowledge and operates in terms of word rather than letter units. Finally phrases rather than words may become the unit and a new spurt of progress occurs. These plateaux in the learning curve are often unduly prolonged because the student becomes discouraged. The teacher can help by explaining this situation.

6. The teacher can suggest the best distribution of time for adequate training. Should learning periods be long? Should we 'strike while the iron is hot' or should we do a little at a time and avoid fatigue? The optimum length for the learning periods will vary from task to task and the teacher should be able to advise. In general it is found that short periods with appreciable rest periods between are most economical. Not only is undue fatigue and boredom avoided, but advantage is taken of an important psychological principle. Long ago, William James, the well known early American psychologist, and incidentally the most readable of all psychological writers, remarked that we learn to swim in the winter and to skate in the summer. He was referring to the fact that we go on improving after we have ceased to practise. The organization of the neural patterns appears to go on after the actual practice period and frequent rests enable us to take the maximum advantage of this. In some cases a better distribution of learning periods may improve learning several hundred per cent.

VERBAL LEARNING

A considerable amount of learning called for at school and college is of the verbal kind. This differs from learning a skill chiefly in that the pattern is already set for us. We do not have to discover what to learn, but merely how to retain it. The very fact that the word pattern is already set may mislead us in our efforts. We may read passively the same passage time and again. This is akin to trying to learn a skill by having our hand or arm guided. It just doesn't work. Teachers have sometimes tried to impart writing skills by guiding the hands of children, but this going through the motions is most unrewarding. In the verbal field an interesting experiment was carried out by requiring a number of subjects to repeat certain number combinations many times. When later asked to repeat these from memory they failed dismally. They had no idea learning might be required and had made no effort to learn. Another group set the task of learning remembered the numbers very well with far fewer exceptions. Mere repetition, like mere practice (without knowledge of results), is useless. Memorizing is usually an *active* process which requires that we *attend* and *intend*. Attention there must be, although this may sometimes be attained by other than voluntary effort.

The active nature of the memorizing process is best illustrated by what is technically known as *recitation*, that is, the attempt to repeat the passage to be learned with prompting where required. The effort to remember maintains a high level of mental arousal and the success obtained by correct repetition is reinforced so that we have a situation very similar to that involved in practising to develop a skill. The attempt at recitation should begin early and not be deferred until the learner thinks he knows the passage. It should be used as a means of learning and not just as a method of testing.

As with learning a skill, memorizing needs to be suitably interspersed with rest periods and the same general principles apply. The nature of the activity during the intervening periods, however, is of some importance. If it is concerned with similar material remembering suffers from what is called *retroactive inhibition*. If the material to be remembered consists largely of names of people and the rest period is occupied with something which requires that we consider a large number of other names, the original names may become lost in the welter of new material.

Complementary to retroactive inhibition is *proactive inhibition* due to the interference caused by previously learned material. A person who very seldom has to remember numbers may easily keep in mind a telephone or house number, but one who is constantly dealing with numerical material may find it essential to rely on a written record. The writer makes a point of listening to the radio weather forecast each day but frequently finds that, if he is questioned about it a few minutes later, very little remains. After all, so many similar forecasts have occurred before. Only if he has reacted to it in terms of 'now I can do so and so' or 'that stops the gardening project' does he remember easily. Recent research has suggested that proactive inhibition is much more important than its retroactive counterpart. This is only to be expected since it is based on a lifetime of preceding experience while retroactive inhibition may be based on only a comparatively short time.

Apart from the question as to how long each memorizing period should be, there is another question as to the size of the learning unit. As children we were inclined to tackle such a task phrase by phrase, repeating it until we thought we knew it and then going on to the next. In contrast to this we may read through a long passage and then re-read it. During a given period we may not succeed at all in memorizing the passage but in time it is remembered as a whole. This is known as the *whole method* as opposed to the *part method* and most evidence has shown that this is the more effective approach, despite the fact that little progress appears to be made at first. The seeming superiority which children find in the part method is largely due to the fact that they are frequently resorting to recitation because they test their progress, whereas they feel that recitation is not called for in the whole method until they have learned the passage. Where recitation is resorted to early in the whole method its superiority is brought out. One advantage is that the passage preserves its essential unity and there is much less likelihood of our losing the link between one part and another as may easily occur with the part method.

PATTERN AND LEARNING

If we have to memorize a meaningless list of words we make very slow progress, but if the words are arranged in meaningful sentences we can quickly memorize a large number. This is because in the sentence the words fall into natural patterns and a group of words may be treated as a unit. The effect is magnified when we come to deal with individual letters. Most people can remember only about six to eight letters after one presentation, but if the letters are presented as members of words in a sentence several dozen may be remembered quite accurately. This is obviously because we have already learned the sub-patterns for the various words as also we have learned phrase patterns. In this way a few key ideas will enable us to remember a whole passage provided it is phrased in familiar terms, because we can reconstruct the sentences fairly accurately. Similarly you can remember a long series of digits if you find they consist of your telephone number followed by the year of your birth, your motor registration number and the year of the Battle of Hastings.

EXTINCTION OF CONDITIONED REFLEXES

When a conditioned response has been established, how permanent is it? Will it disappear in the course of time?

Can we do anything about getting rid of it if we wish? These are rather important questions and they cannot be answered in a few words.

First we have to note that all conditioned responses tend to disappear if the stimulus is presented repeatedly without reinforcement. This is known as *extinction*. It will be remembered that this is an essential part of what we have referred to as differentiation. There are some responses, however, which by their nature make reinforcement impossible, e.g. avoidance responses. If we react to the warning bell and so avoid the electric shock we have no means of knowing whether the shock would have followed or not. We are therefore inclined to equate the absence of the negative reinforcing agent with positive reinforcement and go on repeating the avoidance response indefinitely. The response, however, does tend to become attenuated and finally takes on a token form unless in this process it ceases to be effective and we again experience a shock which causes us to become more careful.

Another factor complicating extinction time is the consistency of reinforcement. If instead of all correct responses being reinforced we reinforce only a fraction of them we find that paradoxically the conditioning becomes more resistant to extinction. Really there is no paradox involved since if we already know that the process works only sometimes we do not suspect that it has ceased to work when it occasionally fails. At first any failure is regarded as only one of the many inconsistencies we have encountered, and so we continue hopefully with our response. How much actual reasoning may be behind it all is unknown, but it would appear that something equivalent to such a reasoning process may occur at quite a primitive level.

Extinction in the case of a drive like fear may present special difficulties. If a child has acquired a fear of mice, repeated presentation of mice without reinforcement may do no more than precipitate chronic anxiety. What is called for is more in the nature of a counter-conditioning process, a positive building up of confidence in such situations. The distant presence of a mouse when other circumstances are strongly reassuring may be tolerated. By keeping the mouse threat small relative to other drive effects, e.g. comforting mother, enjoyable sweets, exciting game, etc., it may be repeatedly presented and with increasing nearness as extinction proceeds. Finally, helped by the example of other children, the child may accept the mouse as a pet.

The consideration of extinction suggests the need for another look at the process of operant conditioning. This has sometimes been considered just the attachment of a response to a drive or even to the stimulus which activates the drive. The process of extinction then becomes the breaking down of this attachment: we build in a link and then destroy it. But the interesting thing is that the extinguished response will very quickly revive if we resort to reinforcement again. It would appear that we do not extinguish the response so much as put it into cold storage.

Mowrer has suggested that the important part of such conditions is not the building of a habit, such as teaching a pigeon to peck at a disk in order to get food, but the attachment of 'hope' or 'fear' to various situations and performances. The pigeon has in fact all the skills necessary for pecking the disk *before* we start the conditioning procedure. What it needs to learn is that such activity is worth while. What it is learning is not the habit but the likelihood of reward. If we reward consistently it will quickly develop a high probability rating of such reward but, correspondingly, non-reward will quickly reduce this probability assessment. With only occasional reward it will (but much more slowly) eventually reach a high probability rating of reward not to a single response but to persistent response. Such a probability assessment will necessarily take much longer also to reduce. In all such cases it is the more recent experience which carries the most weight. So a few recent failures can outweigh many earlier successes and a new success can quickly bring renewed hope which wipes out the effect of recent failures.

All this is exemplified in our rational behaviour. You may have used your telephone a thousand times successfully but you don't wait for a thousand failures before you abandon hope of getting a call through. After a few efforts you desist. But if you have struck gold once you may persist for years before abandoning further efforts. It is interesting to notice that in many cases we find a parallel between the principles operating at the level of conscious thought and at the level of the non-conscious (perhaps we should say 'infra-conscious' rather than 'unconscious') processes. This should be watched for in the case of perception.

It is now possible to summarize the main points with regard to learning principles and relate them to a wider context.

1. Learning involves some kind of bonding process which is doubtless based upon chemical or other changes within the nervous system.

2. This bonding process can involve various elements: sensory, drive, motor. These can appear in various combinations.

3. The term *habit* is best used in connexion with the motor system. A hierarchy of skills is acquired which can be called upon for various purposes.

4. The patterns which underlie our perception are built up in the sensory area. Such patterns are part of the wider *cognitive* system in terms of which we strive to understand our world. Only through such understanding can we carry out the intelligent behaviour on the conscious level whereby we implement our various drives and so manage to live successfully. Much of our learning *is* learning in this cog-

nitive sense. Some psychologists seem to have lost sight of the fact that human behaviour sometimes involves more than a conditioned habit.

5. A very important part of our learning relates to the patterning of drives. This becomes the basis of our motivation system, what is broadly referred to as personality. This is the topic of the next chapter.

6. A very important component in much conditioning may be what Alexander Shand many years ago called a 'derived emotion', one not specific to any particular drive but attaching to all and which ranges from elation, down through various degrees of hope, to complete despair. This concept seems preferable to that of Mowrer which brings in fear as the negative end of this continuum. It is not to be denied that fear does in fact often enter into such situations but it does not necessarily do so. One may lose hope completely in regard to a goal but one does not have to be afraid unless the despair situation is a threatening one. If my goal is to find water on a desert island despair may be associated with fear. But if the goal is to find wild strawberries, despair may involve no fear.

THE AFFECTIVE REFERENCE
FRAME

8

TRAITS AND SENTIMENTS

Our current behaviour may be regarded as stemming from three main sources. First we have simple reflexes in their original and conditioned forms. Secondly we have simple habits which complete themselves in terms of a previously learned sequence. Once a part of the habit has been completed the rest is likely to follow without conscious attention. An amusing instance is that of the person who retires to his bedroom in order to change his clothes and suddenly realizes that he is in his pyjamas ready for bed! We attribute it to absent-mindedness, but by this we refer only to the lack of attention which allows the habit sequence to proceed without correction. The strength of habitual responses is well illustrated by the case of the woman who was suspected of being a male spy. A neat test of sex was made by suddenly throwing something into her lap. Her knees came together smartly to catch the object, thereby revealing that 'she' was accustomed to wearing trousers rather than a skirt. In these days of slacks for women the tests might not be quite so effective.

But habit provides us with only a mechanical kind of behaviour. What we think of as voluntary behaviour falls in the third of the classes we have referred to above, and depends upon the affective reference frame. That is, it derives from basic drives, either directly or indirectly. By the time we are adult little or any of our behaviour can be explained as directly drive-instigated. By this time the drives have been built into systems which enable them to function much more effectively. It is the development of these systems which we now have to study.

PERCEPTUAL CONDITIONING

We have already described perceptual conditioning as a form of learning. We now have to consider in a little more detail the main results of its operation. Where a particular drive has frequently been aroused following a particular stimulus, the latter tends to become the signal for its arousal directly. Thus, if a person frequently provokes us to anger, we tend to be made angry simply by his presence. If we have received several telegrams bearing ill news, the mere sight of the telegraph boy approaching may send our heart into our boots. In such ways we build up a more or less permanent affective attitude towards objects and people. Such attitudes will differ from person to person, depending upon the particular experiences of the person. Usually attitudes change but slowly since they are the result of accumulated conditioning effects, but an unusually intense affective experience may abruptly change the results of long conditioning with milder effects. The writer can still remember how his aesthetically appreciative attitude to certain flowers was suddenly modified by their association with a funeral. For some time he found these flowers distinctly unpleasant.

Because of our varied experiences with objects, and particularly so with people, our attitudes are usually of a rather complex type. Where a number of primary affects are organized around an object or person we have a type of psychological structure that is conveniently referred to as a *sentiment*. The word was first used in this way by Shand and popularized by McDougall early this century. It is an extension of the popular meaning of the word. We speak of something having sentimental value for us, meaning thereby that we have built up an emotional attachment to it. We cherish and care for it; should anyone attempt to injure it we become angry; if it is lost we are sad. Shand and McDougall simply extend this usage of the word. They speak of sentiments of love and hate, or respect, admiration, gratitude, etc. Obviously the number of sentiments of this kind is practically limitless, since we may have not only different combinations of primary affects, but also the presence of these affects in different degrees. Nevertheless, some broad classification of the more common sentiments would appear to be possible, and modern psychologists have perhaps been remiss in not devoting more attention to this area.

The sentiment represents one form of attitude complication: *many affects* organized around an object. Complementary to this we have the generalization of an attitude so that it applies to *many objects*. As an example we have the person who has developed an attitude of timidity to the world in general as the result of his early experiences. Because these have been unfortunate he expects this sort of thing from his world and is biased to a timorous approach to everything. Here we must be careful not to give a wrong impression. An attitude of timidity is usually the product of two factors: inherent capacity of the person for fear and the nature of the fear stimuli he has experienced.

A generalized attitude of this kind is perhaps best described as a *trait*. This word is used by psychologists with a wide range of meanings. Harriman in *The New Dictionary of Psychology* defines it as 'a distinctive pattern of behaviour which is more or less permanent' and gives as examples persistence, introversion, and accuracy. The core of such patterns of behaviour is certainly an affective one and they can be best understood as generalized attitudes as we have defined them here.

Another psychological term should be explained in this connexion. If someone casually calls out a word to you it may suggest a variety of things to you, but if you are told beforehand that you are wanted to think of a word that means the opposite you will probably find that such a word is the first brought to your mind. We say you have a *set* in this direction. If you are engaged in finding rhymes the presentation of a word will evoke another which rhymes with it. If you are waiting to start a race the firing of a gun will launch you into action, but under other circumstances the same sound may produce quite different action. The difference between a set of this kind and an attitude is to be found in the temporary nature of the former. An attitude is based upon a deep-seated affective system and is relatively stable; it should be noted, however, that both terms are frequently used in the literature without any precise meaning beyond that indicated by the given context.

CANALIZATION AND OPERANT CONDITIONING

We have described how operant conditioning results in the building up of appropriate response patterns. We now wish to make a distinction, first suggested by Murphy, which appears to be a useful one. Murphy proposes the word *canalization* for a process which he sees as quite distinct from conditioning. His meaning can best be made clear from an example. A hungry person will seek to eat substances which he recognizes as food. He will select these in terms of his experience of them and, where a choice is possible, he will probably have a well defined scale of priorities. Now it is well known that our choice of foods early becomes restricted in accord with our experience and that we become distinctly averse to unfamiliar foods. Anyone who has travelled much must have been struck by the strange tastes of many foreigners. Most British peoples are very reluctant to eat snails, which are relished in some Continental countries. Such attitudes are undoubtedly acquired and are influenced by factors other than taste. Apart from these factors, however, it is obvious that we do set up a scale of food values in terms of the affective satisfaction enjoyed in eating them. When we have a number of satisfying types of food available our hunger tends to find outlet in one of these directions and we lose interest in further possibilities. These foods come to constitute sub-goals, and it may be said that our hunger drive has become canalized in a number of well defined channels. Now the important difference between such canalization and conditioning is that conditioning depends upon reinforcement for maintenance, but the sub-goal of the canalization is, by definition, always reinforced. The food, because it is a food, always satisfies hunger in some degree. As Murphy points out, you can condition a dog to an electric light but he does not *eat* electric light bulbs!

The process of canalization is part of the wider process of discovering affective values. We have to discover many of the possibilities of affective satisfaction. The sex drive creates tension and a certain degree of direction of activity, but it is by experimentation that the individual discovers really satisfying forms of sex response and the conditions under which this experimentation is carried out may greatly modify the nature of the canalizations finally established. It is for this reason that so many so-called sex perversions exist. Similarly the widespread practice of keeping pets of various kinds might be regarded as a 'perversion' of the parental drive. I venture to suggest that in cultures where children are numerous in all households, there will be very few pets as we know them, although useful animals may be adequately cared for.

The operation of canalization by the *cathecting* * of sub-goals, as we might conveniently describe it in Freudian terms, is very important. These sub-goals may now be pursued by a variety of means. Whereas the cat in the Thorndike box learned (by instrumental conditioning) that a certain motor pattern would enable him to satisfy his hunger the human being may learn (by canalization) that fried

* Cathexis is the attachment of affect to an act or idea.

steak is satisfying when one is hungry and proceed, by whatever means that are at the time most appropriate, to get fried steak or, failing that, some other food high on his scale of priorities. The setting up of such a scale of priorities is a basic step in the building up of value reference frames which are the basis of our voluntary behaviour as distinct from our reflex or conditioned responses.

It should be noted that we are also building up instrumental responses during these periods of experimentation. In the simpler cases these may remain intact as complete conditioned response systems and our behaviour may take place wholly at this level. In other cases, however, the means systems built up may become detached and function as subskills which may be used for a variety of purposes. For example, one may discover how to swim in order to attain a coveted article, and thereafter use swimming for a variety of other purposes. Skills built up in this way are preserved over long periods without reinforcement because they are not stimulated at all and so are not subject to non-reinforcement either. Whenever they are stimulated or brought into use for a specific purpose they are likely to be rewarded and so the patterns tend to be preserved. They belong, however, to the motor systems and not to the value systems with which we are here concerned.

THE DEVELOPMENT OF SENTIMENT

We may gain a better understanding of the nature of sentiments and the important role they may play in motivation if we consider in detail the development of some typical sentiments. The major sentiments relate to people: friend, lover, children, enemy.

Friendship

There are many ways in which friendship can begin, but

always its development can proceed only if it is productive of mutual satisfaction. The need for friends is fundamental and probably related to our security needs. Our early experiences in dependence on parents and other members of the family lead us to seek firm social anchorage for the rest of our lives. As we grow up we seek independence from parental ties and look for increasing support from our peers. This is particularly true in a society which is advancing technically at a rapid rate as is ours. Ways of life change rapidly and parents are naturally regarded as old-fashioned and lacking in understanding of our modern needs. Furthermore, children and adolescents have interests which are naturally different from those of their parents or even in opposition to these, so that they are led to seek mutual support in peer friendships.

Similarity of interest and opinion is important in the development of friendship. To have others approve our opinions adds both to our self-respect (see next chapter) and increases our feelings of security. We thus receive affective satisfaction so that our attachment to our friend is reinforced. This effect is enhanced by what McDougall called the relationship of *active sympathy*. He pointed out that emotion shared is intensified. At least this is true of the pleasurable affects. The reverse is true of painful affect. The proverb has it that we double our pleasures and halve our sorrows by sharing them and ordinary observation seems to confirm this. If we read a good joke we must tell it to our friends. We talk endlessly of our operations. If we are impressed by a play or a picture we insist on inflicting it secondhand on our friends. Anyone who has taken a child to a zoo or a museum will be very familiar with the tendency. 'Oh, come and look at this' is the constant cry, and the demands made on the adult to share experiences may become almost intolerable.

This peculiar enhancement of affective satisfaction which

results from the sharing of experiences provides frequent reinforcement for the developing sentiment. Often our friend can be of material help to us and so bring satisfaction directly in this way. Often we can help our friends, and even this is satisfying to us since it adds to our own feeling of worth-whileness. The outcome of all this is:

1. Our friends become valued as a source of affective enjoyment. We feel that they belong to us in some way. Whatever is a threat to them becomes for that reason a threat to us and we are impelled to fight any such threats. The success of our friends, provided it does not by comparison belittle us, is welcomed as adding to our own prestige. Our friend's sorrows become, in some degree, our sorrows, his joys our joys, his worries our worries.

2. Not only does our friend become valued because he is a source of our own pleasure, but he tends, in some degree, to become valued in his own right, as do our children. The parental drive is a unique source of unselfish behaviour. As already pointed out, survival of the species takes precedence over the welfare of the individual in the evolutionary process, and so most people are so constituted that they will find satisfaction in carrying out behaviour in the interests of the race even if such behaviour is to their personal detriment. It must not be thought for a moment that such behaviour is unselfish in that it does not bring personal satisfaction to the actor. It is, in fact, extremely satisfying usually. Such behaviour is unselfish only in that it is directed towards the welfare of another who is regarded as an end and not a means. It is, in so far as our friends arouse in us something of the tender feeling associated with the cherishing of children, that we become genuinely concerned for their welfare as an end in itself.

Parental love

We have previously discussed the parental drive and its

associated effect. By parental love we mean something more than this. The parental drive leads to the experience of tenderness whenever a suitable stimulus is presented. The response is not specific to a particular object, and when the stimulus disappears it is quickly forgotten. Parental love, on the other hand, is attached to a number of specific objects and is long enduring. It is a powerful source of motivation even after the prolonged absence of its object. The chief contributions to the development of this sentiment are:

1. Even more than friends, children are regarded as one's own. Their good qualities reflect credit on their parents, both as the source of inheritance and of training. On this ground alone parents are likely to feel strongly identified with their children and to react to their welfare as to their own.

2. During infancy the child repeatedly evokes tenderness in the parent so that a strong attitude of tenderness towards the child is formed. This component of the sentiment is very much more in evidence than in the sentiment of friendship. It is here the core of the sentiment and gives this sentiment its special strength. It has been remarked that in times of stress children may sometimes betray their parents, but one never hears of parents betraying their children. Certainly one finds parents occasionally neglecting their children but these are just cases where the sentiment of love has never really developed.

3. As the child grows older it tends to reciprocate the tenderness of the parent and this adds to parental satisfaction.

4. The relationship of active sympathy adds further to the satisfactions and makes a similar contribution as in the case of the sentiment of friendship.

5. Among some people children may be regarded as an insurance against old age and so an important source of security.

It will be noticed that parental love differs from friendship, not so much in the nature of its components, as in their relative importance and particularly in the core position of tenderness. It should be emphasized that the precise form of a sentiment in any individual depends upon his unique experience and that, just as the sentiment of love differs from the sentiment of friendship, so the sentiment of love in one person will differ from the sentiment of love in another.

The sentiment of romantic love

We talk of 'falling in love', but the process is usually slower than this would suggest. Usually it takes time to build up a firm sentiment but various factors may speed up the process. This sentiment involves similar components to those of friendship, but in addition it incorporates the lust drive and may rival parental love in its tenderness component.

Romantic love will frequently begin with a sentiment of friendship. If the partners are sexually attractive a lust component will early be present. In some cases this will overshadow everything else and the friendship components will develop later. Usually tenderness is a major component. When a man falls in love with a girl he is attracted not only by her sexual charms but by her childlike qualities. It is her fragility and dependence on him which arouses his tenderness and inspires him to cherish and protect her. At the same time he has a need to be mothered which evokes her tender emotion. To some extent both partners are finding parent substitutes in the persons of their spouses. To some extent also they are both acting parent roles. This combining of contradictory roles relative to the same object is not an unusual phenomenon and is referred to as *ambivalence*. The more usual antithesis is between love and hate, as we shall see later.

Sometimes there occurs a separation of the lust and tenderness components of romantic love. Because of early experience a person may find it impossible to regard the same person as an object of lust and an object of tenderness. The psycho-analysts have sometimes referred to this condition as 'split libido', libido being the energy of the sex drive. A man suffering from this disability may reverence his wife but be shocked to find her show any interest in sexual intercourse. He himself, however, may seek intercourse with other women whom he considers unworthy of his love. Such women may be valued as a source of satisfaction, but they are not loved. This is an interesting example of how generalized attitudes may influence the development of specified sentiments.

We may now consider what may be involved in 'love at first sight'. Can a sentiment be established so quickly? The answer is probably that the person who so falls in love is strongly influenced by lust stimuli or by tenderness stimuli in the loved person. The basis of this is probably partly innate and partly the result of early conditioning and canalization. That there are some innate elements in sexual attractiveness seems to be evidenced by the way the adolescent's interests normally become directed towards the opposite sex. On the other hand the sort of person found attractive certainly depends upon experience. Most people are attracted by persons of their own race and find those of another race much less attractive. This is certainly the result of experience.

So far as the criteria of physical attractiveness are concerned it is possible that there are two chief norms operating. In the first place we look for typical human form and this is largely determined by the average of our experience. Interesting experiments have been carried out with composite photographs. If one superimposes the negatives of a dozen or more portraits so that a print is produced from the merging of all the individual variations, the result is the picture of a beautiful face! This suggests that the average face is beautiful, which may be rather consoling, but this is not quite the conclusion we can draw. What is required is that all the features of the face should be average. A perfectly good face may be spoilt by a big nose, a receding chin or some other departure from the norm. The second norm is in terms of *difference from* one's own sex and typicality of the opposite sex characteristics. Despite an appreciable incidence of homosexuality in many cultures most people are repelled considerably by anything which suggests homosexual tendencies in themselves, and so require that sexually attractive persons should be obviously of the opposite sex. Some exaggeration of the secondary sex characteristics (e.g. curves in a woman) may be welcomed. A critic said of a certain film star that she had two claims to popularity, both very obvious!

Sometimes certain special conditioning effects operate to make a person specially attractive. In the film *The Man Who Loved Redheads*, the hero falls in love with a succession of girls in the vain effort to recapture a youthful memory. Here we have the transfer of a sentiment rather than the rapid forming of a new one and some cases of love at first sight are undoubtedly of this nature. The sentiment is pre-formed as it were and just becomes attached to an appropriate person.

The sentiment of hate

Hate is in most respects the antithesis of love. Anger is the central element, and tenderness, the central drive in the sentiment of parental love, is absent. It should be noted, however, that anger is organized in the love sentiment since it is aroused whenever the loved person is threatened in any way. It has often been remarked that love easily turns to anger. Anger is the response of any frustration of love, and when the loved person is the source of the frustration, the sentiment of love, particularly of romantic love, may suddenly be converted to one of hate, if only temporarily. Repeated frustration of love in this way will produce an enduring hate sentiment. But of course all hate is not preceded by love. Usually hate begins in its own right and is the result of repeated negative reinforcement. If a person always involves us in unpleasant experiences, such as fear, anger, or pain, we tend to build up a hate sentiment towards him. This, as in the case of love, may be facilitated by previous experience. Most children form sentiments of love towards their parents, but such sentiments tend to be ambivalent, to exist in both positive and negative forms. Children have every reason usually to love their parents since they are the object of so much parental love and care, but also they have every reason to hate the same parents, for parents, by the very nature of their relationship to the child, must be continually frustrating it and arousing its anger. The result is a hate sentiment which alternates with the love sentiment and is potentially present in what the Freudians call 'the unconscious'. As the child develops it may become ashamed to hate its parents and so refuses to give expression to this sentiment except on rare occasions. When someone else frustrates in the way the parents did, however, the hate sentiment may rapidly attach to them, and, since there is no shame attached to it in this context, it may be given uninhibited expression.

This gives some indication of the far-reaching ways our experiences within the family may influence our later behaviour. Not only is passing behaviour influenced but the future developments of the more permanent aspects of the personality may be considerably biased. We shall consider some aspects of this more fully later. At this stage we are chiefly concerned to get some idea of the broad outlines of psychological structure.

9

THE SELF

WE have already noted how the principle of affective control makes human behaviour more elastic and efficient than the reflex or instinctive type of response. We have now to consider the rise to a still higher plane. The affect-controlled response has the great advantage that it provides a goal which can be approached in a variety of ways, according to the circumstances obtaining at the time. It has the weakness of not allowing for conflict of goals or suitability of occasion. A really efficient organism must know when to defer action and when one drive should give place to another. A really satisfactory motivational system must relate to the welfare of the organism as a whole, and relate to it, not merely at the moment, but over the whole life span. It is the achievement of this stage that we are concerned with in this chapter.

The focal point in the motivational system is in this: that when action is related to a unified self, instead of being the function of a passing drive or an automatic reflex response to changing stimulus pattern, we have the possibility of rational and moral behaviour. Rational, not in the sense of being guided by pure reason (a nonsensical notion as we shall see later), but in the sense of conforming in the maximum degree to our affective values. Moral in the sense of securing the welfare, not merely of the individual, but of the race.

It has been pointed out that there are two aspects to the concept of the self, corresponding to the pronouns *I* and *me*. The latter refers to the self as seen by me or by others or by me through others. The former can be only a psychological or philosophical concept. In so far as I view myself it is me which I see and I who do the seeing, but psychologically we can distinguish the *I* which is the focus of experience and action from the *me* which is my concept of myself. It will be convenient for us to refer to the *I* as the *ego* and to the *me* as the *self*. This conforms to the historical development of these two terms, and if the distinction is carefully borne in mind it will save us a lot of confusion.

ESSENTIAL UNITY OF THE ORGANISM

It is worth drawing attention to the fact that the organism does indeed act as a unity in many senses right from the beginning. A pain in any part of the body is *my* pain. We may conceive of it as originating in leg or arm, or even in some cases at no precise place at all, but always it is *I* who feel the pain. A visual scene is seen by me; a sound is heard by me. It is I who smell, or taste, or touch. The general feeling of well-being or depression is my feeling. We cannot conceive of any experience which does not have this ego-reference quality. It would seem, therefore, that we are not called upon to account for the origin of the ego but rather for the particular development which it follows.

Now the development of the ego is intimately tied up with the development of the self. An ego which is related to the experienced moment alone is a poor thing indeed. There must be continuity between the I of one moment and the I of the next, and this must be a known continuity. It is the fact that I know, not only the experience which I am having now, but a whole series of experiences extending back into the past, which makes my 'I-ness' really important, but this is already bringing into the picture some rudimentary ideas of self. As the self grows in richness so does the ego, yet the two do not coincide. We may describe the self as the impression the ego has of itself. This must always be in some degree incomplete and distorted.

THE BODY AND THE SELF

It seems to be well established that the infant does not at first distinguish between its own body and other objects. Its own toes will just be interesting objects for it. It becomes familiar with the world and with itself at the same time, and discovers itself as it discovers the world.

All our understanding of the world has come from our own experiences. It is not just a matter of seeing the world which is there before us. In a sense we never see the world at all. Rather we have experiences, and build up a picture of what the world must be in order to account for these experiences. What we mean by this will be clearer when we deal with the problem of knowing in the next chapter.

Let us consider for a moment the nature of our fundamental experiences. Part of our experience is that of producing motor responses. We move hand or leg, and experience both our innervations and the result of these in terms of pleasant or unpleasant affect. So we early discover that we can control some of our behaviour and that controlling it in one way rather than another produces more satisfactory experiences. This is the first step towards more effective behaviour and we have already described it in the preceding chapter.

In the course of experimenting with various kinds of behaviour we discover our own bodies. Touching a leg is different from touching an object since we experience not only the process of touching but also that of being touched. Experience differences of this kind lead fairly early to the broad distinction of 'my body' from 'the rest of the world', but the boundary is never quite precise. Hair and fingernails may seem part of us in rather a different way from that of arms and legs. They can be removed in part without pain, and certainly seem less vital to us. On the other hand our clothes may often be regarded as an essential part of us, and the way we regard ourselves, and certainly the way in which we consider that other people regard us, depends very much upon our clothes.

WIDENING THE TIME REFERENCE

Our drives in the first place operate directly in terms of the immediate affect experiences. We attempt to satisfy our needs here and now. This is the stage aptly described by Freud as dominance of the *pleasure principle*. The attempt to obtain immediate satisfaction often leads us into difficulties, however, and we learn to await the opportune moment. Learning of this kind may be just a differentiation of conditioning in terms of specific clues (e.g. steaming food may cause experience of burning) or it may be at the level of insight which we have yet to discuss.

Freud described this higher stage of development as control by the *reality principle*. Recent writers frequently use the term '*time binding*' and '*tension binding*' to refer to two aspects of the process. Such terms indicate that the delay in responding is dependent on insight rather than on conditioning. This stage is not begun until about the end of the first year and is largely a social product.

In civilized society the child has few opportunities to experience what some educators have called 'the punishment of natural consequences'. He learns to avoid the hot fire, not because of the experience of being burned, but because of the disapproval of adults. Adult disapproval with punishment or the threat of punishment is very frequent during the early years, since the child has to be prevented from doing, not only acts which may have harmful consequences to himself, but also those which may have harmful consequences to adults, e.g. breaking a vase or scratching the piano. Repeated disapproval by adults plays the major part in bringing about time and tension binding. The child learns to delay action, to look before it leaps. This is certainly a grave step in the development of the ego. In fact Freud regarded this as the origin of the ego, but such a view would not be accepted today outside psycho-analytic circles.

THE SOCIAL CODE

The presence of a social factor introduces a very important complication into the learning process. Because the child has to depend on parental tenderness for its fundamental security and the satisfaction of its physiological needs, the parents wield an enormous power. The child must always take their likely reactions into consideration. At first he may find their interference quite arbitrary, but there is usually some consistency behind it all and this slowly becomes evident. The child learns something of the code involved. Very early he comes to judge both himself and others in terms of the parental code. He will scold a brother or sister, not only for the same shortcomings, but in the same tone of voice as that used by the parent. He will scold himself for similar shortcomings. At first the self-scolding may be just an accompaniment of the forbidden activity, which is seemingly not hindered by it, but careful observation shows that the child is experiencing something of a conflict and the sudden appearance of an adult may throw it into confusion.

A little later we may find the same child admonishing himself when about to perform the disapproved action, and then desisting. What has happened is that he has been able to represent to himself the disapproving attitude of his parents to this activity and to take this into consideration. Threatened loss of parental approval has aroused his *anxiety,* which constitutes a more potent drive than the satisfaction of a passing impulse such as to eat the jam.

In this connexion we should observe that there are two types of approach which the parent may make in bringing about conformity of this kind. He may punish the child directly for non-conformity by smacking, taking away a favourite toy, or depriving of some privilege. On the other hand he may not punish directly but just 'appeal' to the child. This latter approach is possible only if the child has experienced a strong supportive attitude from the parent. The child seeks love from its parents and any interference with this situation is anxiety provoking. For this reason it has been suggested that parents should avoid this kind of control. It has to be acknowledged, however, that this is the source of conscience and it may be that we can go too far in our enthusiasm to avoid anxiety. A little anxiety may be necessary to a healthy social group.

It is worth noticing that children who are most punished are often the most disobedient. It may be that they are punished because they *are* disobedient, but careful study does not seem to bear this out. Clinical studies of severe behavioural problems frequently reveal that the child has felt rejected by its parents and deprived of the parental love it craved. It has then sought to gain attention by being naughty, or has relinquished the hope of getting love and has become hard and defiant. Punishment has then become something to be avoided if possible, but something to be accepted as a necessary evil if it cannot be avoided. It is impossible to appeal to the better nature of such people because they have rejected the very basis of this.

At this stage we must stop for a while to consider the nature of anxiety. Sullivan* suggests that this originates in the fear communicated to the child by the emotional disturbance of the mother. The social communication of fear

* H. S. Sullivan, *An Interpersonal Theory of Psychiatry*, pp. 8–12.

is a common phenomenon among many birds and animals, and is no doubt related to the protective advantage conferred on a species when its members take to flight on perceiving the fear expressions of any one member and do not wait to experience the original fear stimulus directly. One bird takes to flight and immediately all birds in the vicinity are also in headlong flight. In this way the younger birds acquire valuable fear cues. In the same way we have noted that children acquire fear of mice and similar fears. But if the mother shows manifest fear without taking refuge from a specific object the child experiences a fear sensation which it cannot relate to any specific danger. Such fear experiences are particularly disturbing and suggest a threat to the child's basic security.

Now we may point out that our feeling of security depends upon two factors. Firstly there is our knowledge of how to handle the stimuli to which we are exposed, our general know-how of existence. In so far as we find ourselves in a familiar situation where we can satisfy our needs through familiar response system, we feel confident that we can deal with things. Even a known danger will not unduly upset us provided it does not get out of hand. If we are able to meet it we are not deeply disturbed. But any suggestion that our response patterns are no longer effective is profoundly upsetting, and this may be so although no known danger is threatening. If our world is no longer the one which we have come to understand, anything may happen and danger is certainly just round the corner. Under these conditions we may experience anxiety of varying degrees, sometimes assuming panic proportions.

The second source of our security is in the feeling of social support. Primarily we depended upon the care of our parents, who were able to shield us from all dangers. As we grew older and were able somewhat to fend for ourselves we could always fall back on parental help when our resources failed. Parental support gradually widened its sphere to take in the support of all adults and others who were favourably disposed to us. Because of this key part played by parents in the building up of our security, it is easy to see how fear responses in the parents, unaccompanied by effective action, could build up strong anxiety and how any suggestion of parental rejection could strike a blow at the whole edifice of personal security.

With such a powerful drive behind it one can easily see how the child would be impelled to behaviour which would retain this feeling of parental support, and it is possible that this factor alone would be sufficient to establish the parental code of behaviour in the child, but there are probably other factors at work too. Anyone who has had experience with children will have noted how enthusiastically they respond to approval. Particularly is this so when they have succeeded, often with considerable effort, in carrying out a new action. It seems obvious that they delight in their new mastery and that this delight is magnified by social approval. That not merely social approval is involved is evidenced by the fact that, when the act is disapproved, it will still be repeated with glee until the social disapproval becomes too strong to be ignored. It is quite possible that achievement is innately endowed with positive affect and that success in achieving any goal is satisfying irrespective of whether it is related to a specific drive or not. In fact this might be considered to be a drive itself, should we say a 'mastery' or 'achievement' drive. It would be very difficult to prove the existence of such a drive and nobody has made any serious attempt to do so, but there is considerable evidence that, in Western society at least, people do manifest varying degrees of achievement need. This is doubtless related to the early delight in achievement manifested by the child and strongly reinforced by parental and general social approval.

The urge to achieve, which is thus fostered by social approval, finds its direction also determined by the same social factor. What is approved by society is not the momentary action but the *person*, and so we come to consider each of our actions as contributing to make us more or less the sort of person who will be socially approved. One action may have little effect, but a long series of meritorious deeds may raise our stock to high levels on the social market. It is here that the self concept becomes really important, because this is just our evaluation of our own person. It might be said that it is ourself as we see ourself through the eyes of other people.

THE SELF-IDEAL

In the preceding pages we have tried to show how the ego gradually becomes aware of itself, first as a continuing reference point, a focus of experience extending back into the past through its memories, secondly as a bodily entity, and finally as a behaving organism carrying out actions which are evaluated by others, primarily by the parents, and endeavouring to enhance the self in terms of the reference frame established. We have tried to explain all this in terms of two concepts: ego and self. But, although these are distinct as concepts, they both refer to the same entity. It is always the ego which acts. The self simply constitutes a reference frame with regard to which the ego orders its action, but it is not the only reference frame involved. In fact we might conveniently distinguish three reference frames of this nature:

The ideal personality, a level of perfection which I cannot even hope to achieve.

The ideal self, the sort I hope to be. In experimental studies the phrase *level of aspiration* has been much used. When set a task to do, such as cancelling all the letter 'e's' in a text, or of coaxing ball-bearings through a hole, subjects vary considerably in their estimates of what they will achieve. Some will set their goal considerably above their eventual achievement, while others will be much more modest in their hopes. Such discrepancies in level of aspiration may continue even after many trials. Similarly we find great differences among people with regard to the self-ideal to which they aspire. Such differences, however, are not determined by the same factors as operate in the case of specific tasks such as those we have referred to above. Some psychologists have written as though they assumed this to be the case, and certainly some of the factors are likely to be in common, but there are likely to be some important differences too. One of these differences will be that the self-ideal will not be just a matter of degree but often more a matter of specific content (e.g. give precedence to a lady), and much of this content will be common to most members of the social group.

The actual self seen as achieving or falling short of the self-ideal. In the former case there is the glow of achievement; in the latter case there is regret or remorse, which in extreme cases may be so acute as to motivate suicide, as in the case of the Japanese gentleman who has failed to live up to traditional requirements. Where honour is lost life may have lost all value for us.

SELF ASPIRATION

Self aspiration may be thought of as falling into two distinct spheres:

Material

This depends to a considerable degree on ability and good fortune. We might like to be world-famous poets or scientists, but, if we are but poorly equipped with abilities we may early have to resign any such aspirations. Usually we can relinquish such impossible goals without undue disturbance since we cannot be held accountable for the lack of such abilities. In other cases we may relinquish aspirations despite the fact that we have considerable aptitude because, as William James so aptly pointed out,* we cannot hope to achieve all kinds of success and some goals are mutually incompatible anyway. One cannot be both a scholar and a man of action who despises books. We, therefore, have to choose some alternative goals, and when we have chosen we may be happy to confess the grossest incompetence in the rejected areas of achievement. The famous astronomer may be in no degree perturbed by the fact that he cannot remedy a simple fault in his motor-car.

Moral

Although it may be recognized that there are moral heights which few can scale there is a general feeling that, whereas material achievement is dependent on capacities which are not common possession, moral achievement is within the compass of everybody. Psychologists would consider this an unwarranted assumption, but the fact that it is made is very important for behaviour. Furthermore there is some basis for the assumption. For most people social approval does come to be the greatest of all needs, and so they will carry out the actions which will retain and increase such approval. In terms of their social experience they set up a moral level of aspiration in terms of an ideal self which they constantly endeavour to achieve.

MORAL ACTION AND THE WILL

Early psychology paid considerable attention to a concept known as *will*, but the recent period has tended to regard the whole notion as outmoded. Latterly, however, related concepts have made an appearance, and with the return of

* William James, *Psychology* (Briefer Course), Macmillan and Co., London, 1892, p. 186.

the self to respectability, the notion of will may be given some sort of scientific explanation. The older ideas of will suggested that it was some sort of super-material entity which required performance to which the weaker flesh was averse. The material body might wish to embark on its sensual enjoyments, but the spiritual will sternly forbade. Scientific study found no evidence for such a spiritual entity and dismissed the idea as just another superstition. Once again, however, we are finding that the quaint notions of our ancestors are quaint in their garb rather than in their underlying principles. What impressed these early thinkers was that we so frequently appear to act 'in the line of greatest resistance', as William James described it. We seem obviously to do things which we dislike. We stay at home to do disagreeable chores when we might be enjoying golf or swimming. We drag ourselves from an exciting book to dry the dishes, although we may hate the task. We may risk death to help a friend, or we may go bravely to the stake to defend our religious beliefs. What explanation can we offer for all this in terms of the psychological principles we have so far sketched? The answer is not far to seek: we forgo possible pleasures because they do not fit into the self system. To yield to them would be to accept an inferior self and more than outweigh any immediate pleasure. We therefore choose the hard way, what seems to be the line of greatest resistance. In fact we are taking the longer view and building up for ourselves a greater amount of net pleasure. Weaker egos may be tempted to pay for their errors later. The strong ego with a well-integrated self and self-ideal manifests its 'will power'. It is interesting in regard to this that Cattell, in his recent factorial analysis of personality, finds a factor which he names *will control* and which seems to provide direct empirical evidence of what we have described here and which seems to underlie the old concept of a 'strong will'.

A later chapter will discuss further this question of control by the will and it will be argued that this is an important measurable dimension of personality despite its close relationship to the self-sentiment. There is, however, a further possibility: that the moral aspect of the self-sentiment may in fact need to be split into two factors. One of these may depend upon moral ideals, a striving for superiority in moral attributes, and the other perhaps have the more specific qualities of the super-ego, perhaps best thought of in terms of duty and obligation. It is possible that religious concepts may play an important part with regard to the latter. It is certainly true that with many people much of the content of the super-ego is religiously based but whether this is necessarily so or whether we should have a separate super-ego factor even without any religious teaching is something on which it would be difficult to pronounce in the present state of our knowledge.

EGO-INVOLVEMENT

The importance of the self and the self-ideal is illustrated in another connexion. At a children's picnic parents may be induced to race, with many of them putting up a very poor performance and yet seemingly little worried by their lack of success. A poet, posed a mathematical question, may not even attempt to answer and again be in no way dismayed, although a mathematician who failed to answer, or answered wrongly, might blush with shame. Obviously it all depends upon what we have at stake. Most poets have few mathematical pretensions and neither expect nor imagine other people will expect a high mathematical performance from them. For the mathematician, on the other hand, it is a very different matter. Mathematical achievement is part of their self-ideal, or, in other words, they are *ego-involved* in this respect. This idea of ego-involvement is quite an important one. It probably accounts for some of the deficiency of elderly people in working intelligence tests. For many of them there is no ego-involvement. It is a school type of task and nobody could expect them to do well. Failure, therefore, does not matter.

Lack of ego-involvement, however, does not necessarily mean there is no motivation. There may be motivation at a lower level. I may attempt to get a meal at a restaurant known to me and if I find that it is closed I shall feel frustrated and annoyed because my hunger still requires satisfaction. Yet, if the closing is quite unexpected, say because of sickness of the proprietor, I find no reflection on my self. I am not ego-involved as I should probably be in passing an examination. Here, to fail would be a reflection on me, would suggest that I am an inferior person, and I should experience, not merely a passing annoyance, but a profound depression. It is characteristic of such depression that one tends to devalue all one's previous achievement. Every previous failure, however insignificant, may be remembered and we may be quite convinced that we are just no good, destined to be a failure in life. This widespread effect is doubtless because it is not just one of our actions which has failed, but rather the organized self-system. Our self-stock has fallen, just like the shares of a company which has received an adverse report. Correspondingly, success which involves the self in this way produces a widespread and continuing exhilaration. After passing a similar exam with high honours we may find ourselves 'walking on air' for several days and viewing life through rose-coloured glasses.

CONSCIENCE VERSUS SOCIETY

A paradox which a psychological theory of morals has to face is the fact that we sometimes find people acting on moral principles which are not in accord with society. Our moral reformers have always been in danger of being stoned or crucified by their contemporaries. Conscientious objectors to military service are certainly not all physical cowards. Some of them have distinguished themselves by outstanding bravery. Where do such people acquire a self-ideal which is in conflict with social standards? There appears to be a reasonable answer to this question. A study of such people shows that they are always concerned with approval, but this approval is that of a more enlightened society or of God Himself. They are convinced that future generations will applaud their action, and certainly this has frequently happened. History is full of such instances.

McDougall has remarked that the rise to this higher plane of morality is facilitated by the presence of a number of moral codes. The child finds that the social group in which he finds himself after leaving home has different standards from those of his parents, and that other groups have still other standards. Under these conditions he may become cynical and simply adjust his behaviour to the code of the social group in which he usually finds himself, or he may be led to search for some higher standard. He may find the standards of some groups higher than those of another and choose the highest standard available or he may go beyond existing groups and look for the approval of an ideal society. Thus the very factors which led him earlier to accept the social code now lead him to oppose the same code. There seems to be nothing illogical about this.

THE COGNITIVE REFERENCE FRAME

10

PERCEPTION

Stare at the picture below for several minutes. You will probably find that, although you recognized it at once, it suddenly changes as you look at it and you recognize a totally different object. As you continue to look you will find that it alternates between these two interpretations.

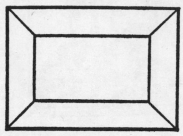

Fig. 4.

Now look at Figure 5. Here, again, you will get immediate recognition but discover after a while that the same alternating phenomenon takes place. Note the length of time be-

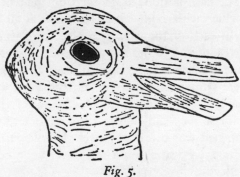

Fig. 5.

tween changes by counting slowly and notice whether one form tends to come more easily than another. Try to hurry or delay changes.

Here is a third one which you may find more difficult but which will certainly change if you give it time. When the change does come it is quite a dramatic one.

Fig. 6.

In each of the above cases you were presented with a stimulus pattern to which you attributed meaning. The fact that you found two meanings in each case is very important. The case is quite different from that of a vague stimulus which we are unable to recognize at all with any certainty. In each of the examples here there was a clear, definite perception. You did not guess what it might be, but *saw* it quite clearly just as you would see an actual object. It was there with considerable detail, and then, quite suddenly, you had a different perception, equally clear. The process was not due to any logical consideration of evidence. What happened was below the level of consciousness. The waving of a fairy wand could not have produced a more dramatic effect.

This changing of the perception while the stimulus pattern remains the same poses quite a problem, and we have introduced it here to dispel a naïve illusion about perception. Common sense assumes that there are things in the world and that we just see them. It is much more complicated than that. What we are presented with is a stimulus pattern, and it is from this stimulus pattern that we try to reconstruct reality. We have said *reconstruct*, because we assume that reality is there in the first place, but we have to be very careful to remember that we cannot compare our reconstruction with reality itself because *we never know it except through our stimulus patterns*. For this reason reality must always be for us an assumption, usually a pretty well substantiated one, but nevertheless never something absolute and always something we may have to modify in terms of further experience.

The subjective nature of perception is well brought out by consideration of colour. As the writer looks out of his window now he sees green trees and houses painted cream, green, red, grey, and white. A colour-blind person would see a very different scene and colour-blind people are not uncommon (about three per cent of men have an appreciable degree of colour-blindness). Does the writer or the colour-blind person see the real thing? The usual assumption is that the colour-blind person is missing something of reality, just as the blind man is missing much more. Physicists tell us, however, that what we speak of as colour is more objectively to be described as a particular wave-length of light. All these variations in wave-length can be represented on a single continuum with only quantitative differences. The qualitative differences which we call colour are added by us in much the same way as the electrician uses different coloured wires to avoid confusion. It seems quite clear that colours as qualitatively different are a function of the organism and not of the environment, the world of reality outside us. Confirmation of this is to be found in the fact that some people associate colour with *hearing* as well as seeing.

This discussion of colour will have emphasized that perception is always dependent upon both subject and environment. If the experiencing organism changes, so does its perception (e.g. loss of colour receptors). Likewise, if the environment changes, the perception changes. But, of course, the experiencing organism is also a part of reality, so that changes of either kind are to be related to changes in reality ultimately. What we have to keep clear is that we *infer* rather than *see* reality. By way of further evidence consider solidity. Certain objects certainly appear solid to us, and yet our visual stimuli all have to be transmitted through the two-dimensional retina. How, then, do we come to experience a third dimension of depth? We shall consider this in more detail later, but here we may note we can get this third-dimensional effect also from two-dimensional films, and to some extent from a simple picture on a flat surface. The presence again of an inferential process is evident.

Let us now return to the alternating perceptions we had with the illustrations at the beginning of this chapter. It should be noted that, although we think of a cube or a rabbit as having a fixed and definite form, yet we seldom receive the same perceptual pattern from either twice. A cube has six sides, but we never see six sides because one at least is always hidden. These sides are all the same size, but they can never all be the same size in the stimulus pattern because of the perspective effects. In fact, we see every object in a multitude of ways but all these are consistent with a particular interpretation. If the cube is, in fact, six-sided, etc., we can expect to see all the variations we do, and therefore we refer each of our experiences to a common reality. But it can happen that a particular stimulus pattern

from a rabbit's head can be very similar to a particular
stimulus pattern from a duck's head. Under these circumstances we may be torn between two possible interpretations. So, also, two different positions of a cube may have
the same outline representation, with again competing interpretations. Since in a picture not all detail is included, it is
possible for an artist to leave out certain details which might
favour one interpretation rather than another, and so we
get a really ambiguous figure.

Let us look at a further picture. On this page is a picture
of an object to be seen through a small peep-hole at Prince-
ton University. The actual object is hidden from the casual
gaze by a large box. As seen through the peep-hole it is
quite obviously a chair, but when we are taken to the back

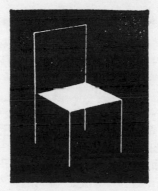

Fig. 7.

of the box and allowed to look through the trapdoor a
very different scene meets our eyes. A picture of this is
shown on the next page. It is most obviously not a chair and
we are puzzled to account for our ever seeing it as a chair.
Obviously there is one position in which this conglomeration produces the same stimulus pattern as does an actual

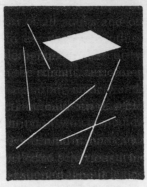

Fig. 8.

chair and our perceptual functioning seizes on this interpretation.

THE STIMULUS PATTERN

Let us now consider the nature of the stimulus patterns which underlie our perception. We cannot understand how the *cognitive* (i.e. knowing) *reference frame* is built up unless we know the nature of the raw material which underlies it. We are equipped with a number of sense organs which are sensitive to stimuli of various kinds: the eye is sensitive to light, the ear to air vibrations, the tongue to certain chemical stimuli, the nose to olfactory stimuli which may produce a chemical reaction or may, possibly, operate through varying wave-lengths of heat absorption. The latter theory is of fairly recent origin. It would make smells parallel to colours. The skin records heat, cold, pressure, and pain. In the ear is also the balance-recording mechanism to which we have already referred. Finally, we receive sensation from within the body, informing us of pains, pressure, and limb movements.

It should be noted that, although our senses are sensitive to a considerable range of stimuli, we have evidence for the existence of stimuli which do not register on them. The electrical waves propagated by radio stations are quite without effect on us until converted into sound by our radio receiver. The physicist finds that these waves belong to the same series as light (400–750 billion cycles per sec.), but our senses are responsive only within certain limits. So again for air or mechanical vibrations. Below 20 cycles per second we cannot hear them, but may experience them as pressure. Above 20,000 cycles per second practically everybody is insensitive, although dogs may go much higher, and bats are continually making use of sounds well above the human limit. Again the physicist is familiar with cosmic rays to which all our sense organs are insensitive. It is quite clear, therefore, that the human being with all his senses in good condition is still receiving only a fraction of available stimuli and must infer the rest.

Most of our sense organs provide data of a very simple kind and we need not here concern ourselves very much with their mechanism. Vision and hearing, however, are somewhat more complicated and need a little more consideration of the nature of their data. First we must distinguish a noise from a musical tone. Both depend upon vibration communicated to the ear, but the vibrations in the latter case are regular. A graphic representation of the difference makes it clear:

Noise   *Tone*

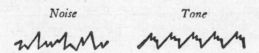

Fig. 9. *Tones differ in pitch* (*corresponding to frequency*) *and both noise and tone may vary in loudness* (*corresponding to amplitude of waves but influenced also by frequency*).

It will be seen, then, that we may have a very considerable variety of patterns, even when we restrict ourselves to the tones, which are the basis of our music, since we may have, indeed cannot avoid, varying combinations of pure tones so that the same note sounded by two different musical instruments is quite different. But, when we allow for the various noise possibilities too, the range becomes enormous.

This range of auditory patterns makes it possible for us to recognize many things in terms of the sounds which they emit. So we recognize the cat and the dog, the car and the train, the voice of a friend on the telephone, but auditory patterns usually permit little more than recognition. Hearing a strange animal for the first time may give little indication of what the animal is like. Certainly a big noise may suggest a large animal and a tiny squeak suggest a small one, but even this may be misleading, and important matters like shape are in no way indicated. Vision, on the other hand, provides us with considerably more detail. We have a good indication of size. We see horns, claws, or teeth, and we note the friendly attitude or the threatening gesture. It is quite obvious why vision should be our preferred sense and why seeing tends to be equated with understanding.

The outstanding advantage of vision is that it provides data in two dimensions. Actually we appear to see three dimensions but the monocular sensory pattern is in two dimensions only. Light shines through the lens of the eye and forms a pattern on the curved surface of the retina at the back of the eye, much as the lens of the camera produces an image on the film in the camera. This two-dimensional pattern is conducted to the brain by a network of nerves and provides the data for our visual perception, and is usually in terms of both colour and brightness variations, depending upon the nature of the light wave-lengths reflected from the object and the degree to which they are reflected.

INTERPRETING STIMULUS PATTERNS

We have now to see how the raw data of sensory input come to have meaning for us and how we build up our picture of the world. We say that we know our world and so can find our way about in it intelligently. In fact we are limited to certain patterns of neurological stimulation, and, in some marvellous way, manage to build up for ourselves that convincing picture of reality with which we are all familiar. It is fascinating to consider how all this may be achieved.

We have already stressed that perception is dependent both on the nature of the outside world and the nature of the individual. It should be pointed out, however, that the individual is himself part of this world and that he owes his continued existence to the effectiveness of his coping with this world. His perceptual equipment has been evolved in terms of its usefulness in relating him to the world and so, on the whole, we may expect that it will lead to a more correct rather than to a distorted view of reality. With this warning let us consider some of the innate perceptual factors.

INNATE AND LEARNED PERCEPTUAL FACTORS

Channel Limitation

We are accustomed to thinking of visual patterns as similar to pictures, with all the intimate detail which is normally present in a picture. This is misleading. Our retina is so constructed that it records accurately at the point of focus (the *fovea centralis*, where the cone nerve cells which mediate vision in normal light are closely bunched together) but with increasing vagueness as we get away from the focal point. This means that we must concentrate on one area at a time. Apart from this there appears to be a limit to the amount of information which can be handled at any given moment, in much the same way as there is a limit on the number of cable messages which may be transmitted simultaneously from one station. Items of information are measured in terms of 'bits'. Each bit corresponds to a yes or no answer to a question, and it is found that the average person can handle only about three bits at a time. Three bits will enable us to record any number up to seven (*yes four* plus *yes two* plus *yes one*), and we find that people can count about seven items in a single glance, repeat about seven numbers or letters after a single hearing, and so on. But if we can take in only about seven items at a time, even of the simplest nature, why can we look at a complicated scene and register trees, houses, animals, men, etc., when even a single house involves many items (doors, windows, roof, spouting, etc.)? The answer is in terms of perceptual learning.

Perceptual learning

The young aeroplane enthusiast catches a momentary glimpse of a plane and is able to explain that it is of a particular type and has such and such details of construction. He will probably be able to sketch its appearance for you, and generally manifests a striking knowledge of all kinds of detail about it. Of course this knowledge was not obtained from the mere glimpse. This merely enabled him to note a few clues (say three bits of information!) but these were sufficient to bring about recognition. In fact he may be able to recognize seven such planes at once. G. A. Miller expresses the matter most effectively by making a distinction between bits of information and 'chunks' of information. We shall discuss later why a chunk can be handled in much the same way as a bit. At this stage we shall merely emphasize that perceptual learning takes place in such a way as to bind bits of information into a system, and that, by making use of such systems, we are able to perceive complex patterns which would otherwise be quite beyond our capacity. This is well brought out by comparing the result of glancing along a line of printed words in our own language and then glancing in a similar way at a line of Greek or Hebrew characters. If we are not familiar with these latter languages such a glance leaves us with just nothing we can report unless we concentrate on a single letter. Even when we have spent some time learning a foreign language we are apt to complain that the natives speak too quickly. We are unable to perceive the spoken words adequately because we have not yet built up an appropriate knowledge of language 'chunks'. We need to perceive each word separately, whereas the person who is really familiar with the spoken language recognizes a whole phrase at once. At this stage we probably find we can read the language much faster than we can comprehend the spoken form because we have probably had much more training in recognition of the written form. A person who has learned the language by the so-called direct method may show decided superiority in oral conversation just because his learning has been so much with the spoken form.

Figure–ground effect

When a part of the visual field is different in colour or shade from the rest, it is perceived as a figure with the rest appearing as ground. The smaller area always tends to be the figure, but, when the areas begin to approach balance, the position tends to become unstable. This is well illustrated in the case of the Peter–Paul goblet shown in Fig. 10. Usually the goblet is perceived first but if one focuses on the thin stem of the goblet two profiles appear and the white becomes background. Although one can influence this change to some degree it persists in alternating for most people. The dramatic nature of the change which takes place emphasizes

Fig. 10.

that there is a complete reorganization of the visual field. It should be noted, also, that detail is observable in the portion regarded as figure whereas the background tends to be rather homogeneous.

Innate grouping effects

A German group of psychologists known as the *Gestalt school* have brought to our attention several laws according to which objects tend to be grouped:

1. *Similar objects tend to be grouped together.* Below we see two rows of noughts and two rows of crosses. If the page is turned round we now see coloumns instead of rows. The similarity of the noughts causes them to be grouped together and the crosses to appear in another grouping.

o o o o o
x x x x x
o o o o o
x x x x x

Fig. 11.

2. *Proximity favours grouping.* The six lines in Fig. 12 appear as three pairs. This grouping is quite spontaneous

and is doubtless in terms of neurological tensions, and, perhaps, just another aspect of the figure–ground tendency. Our understanding of psychological effects such as these is considerably hampered by lack of neurological knowledge, but considerable research is going on in this area and there are already signs of increasing understanding.

//   //   //

Fig. 12.

3. *Common movement favours grouping*. This tendency cannot be illustrated very effectively in a diagram, but it is easy to find an example. If several figures are drawn on a window-pane and the head moved slowly from side to side while looking through the glass, the figures drawn there will appear to move together and so tend to form a group. A similar effect can be obtained by superimposing a sheet of transparent paper on another. Movement of one sheet at once causes the marks on it to assume a separate pattern.

4. *Meaning effort*. The outstanding feature of all perception is the effort to attain meaning. Such meaning is evident at once in clear perception of such things as chairs, books, pens, and other familiar objects. In a darkened room, however, we may be uncertain, and then we find ourselves guessing, not consciously, but at the perceptual level. An indistinct object appears to be one thing and may then appear to be something else, the change taking place as in the examples of reversible figures at the beginning of this chapter, but we do see *something* and not just a vague pattern.

We might argue that the whole point of perception is meaning, and that to perceive without finding meaning would not really be to perceive at all. This is a crucial point and requires further elaboration. What in fact do we mean

143

by 'meaning'? This is a question which has led to much disagreement.

MEANING AND MEANS

We have earlier spoken of drives and the means by which they could be satisfied. It may strike the reader as a somewhat unexpected relation but we would suggest that a thing has meaning in so far as it is recognized as a means. It is interesting to note that young children tend to define things in terms of their function, e.g. 'a spoon to eat with', 'a chair to sit on'. Such definitions may appear to us to be rather crude, but they highlight the essential meaning.

The rat in the Skinner box presses a lever and obtains food, thereby satisfying his hunger. The lever is the means to his satisfaction, and thereby has meaning. The bars of his cage prevent his escape, and they too have meaning, although in a negative sense. At this level of behaviour the means relates directly to the goal, but with more complex behaviour the means may involve a series of steps. To take a simple case, we may get into a car and drive to a restaurant. Driving to the restaurant has meaning in relation to hunger satisfaction, but notice that the car is only one link in the chain and may be a step in several other chains of action, e.g. visiting the girl friend. We can now think of the motor-car in relation to other *means* rather than as in relation to a particular end such as eating. We say, then, that we understand its meaning in so far as we know how it relates to these other means, or part-means. So the meaning of a spanner relates to its function in turning nuts. Nevertheless, any such function has significance only in terms of wider function and, ultimately, in so far as it contributes to the achievement of a drive-goal.

But, having emphasized that these two aspects of meaning are ultimately related to the same thing, drive satisfaction, we are now ready to confess that it may be useful to distinguish between them, using for this purpose the terms 'affective meaning' and 'cognitive meaning'. By the latter we refer to the relationship of our perceptual units. By our cognitive activity we reduce our world to a system of relationships through the understanding of which we are able to find the means to our drive-goals. Our cognitive activities become like building blocks with which we can construct various devices according to our needs.

We may regard the problem of perception thus: the problem of coding the universe in a representational system which will enable us to carry out appropriate actions to satisfy our needs. The satisfactory carrying out of this coding process is satisfying in its own right because of our exploratory drive. It is because we get this drive satisfaction from understanding things that we are able to build up a satisfactory cognitive reference frame which will always be ready to serve us in the satisfaction of our specific drives. Of course, we could build up a cognitive reference frame without curiosity, but it would be rather restricted and would perhaps consist more of a number of separate reference frames relating to our major drives and with very little relation between one reference frame and another. Curiosity leads us to attempt to make one consistent reference system out of the lot. In so far as we succeed we feel some mastery over our environment, some security in our world.

We have referred to coding the universe. We must now explain that such coding is not merely a matter of translating into another form as when we change a verbal message to a set of figures. The essential part of the process is conversion of sensory stimuli into more manageable form. This is made necessary by our three-bit perceptual span. We have already given some indication of how suitable coding may enable us to surmount this restriction. We now need to consider the matter more carefully. The possibilities may be made clear by reference to our number system. If we have to convey the idea of three rabbits we may speak of one rabbit, another rabbit, and still another. We thus need as many code units as we have rabbits. By resort to numbers we can refer to the three units by a single symbol: 3. We have different symbols to refer to each quantity up to ten. Above this we resort to a new economy. We refer to the number of tens plus the number of units, and so can denote any number below a hundred by the use of two symbols. By now using the same set of symbols we can denote a number up to a thousand by using only three symbols, and so on. This is an enormous economy, but it does not stop here. If we wish to use really big numbers such as 1,000,000,000, we may resort to a further economy and just write 10^9, i.e. 10 to the 9th power, 1 with nine noughts following.

The reader may find this quite impressive but fail to see how it can apply to the problem of perception, since in numbers we are concerned just with the repetition of similars while perception has to deal with a multiplicity of different things. The principles underlying our written language offer a more helpful parallel. Each letter involves a visual pattern sufficient to tax our visual span when first met. Several such patterns constitute a word but we frequently find that it is easier to recognize a long word than it was at first to recognize a single letter. It may be objected, however, that we are here concerned with memory rather than perception. To this we must answer that perception *depends* upon memory. A long word printed in strange characters is seen as just a meaningless jumble of marks. Really to perceive it we have to look in turn at each letter. Each of these has to be perceived as combinations of vertical, horizontal, and oblique strokes linked together with curves of various kinds since these are the only units which we have experienced before and so have meaning for us. These are the units supplied from our memory. But when we have 'learned' the letters we are able to see them at once as units and do not need to concern ourselves with strokes. And when we are familiar with the words we see them at once and do not need to concern ourselves with the letters. This is emphasized by the experience we have of reading a passage and failing to notice a misspelled word or a missing letter. We recognized the word or phrase and 'saw' what ought to be there.

In the next chapter we shall be concerned with the actual nature of the perceptual coding system and how it is built up. Some of the principles involved here have been known for a long time; some are highly speculative and only just being investigated, but we shall try to present a coherent and meaningful picture in the light of present development.

11

PERCEPTUAL LEARNING

BEFORE we attempt to describe stages in the process of perceptual learning there is one important point which should be mentioned. We have referred to the three-bit limit on our perceptual intake. This can be increased if we are prepared to sacrifice accuracy. In a brief exposure we can note accurately the presence of only about seven units, but we may make a rough estimate of a hundred or more. These more extensive but more vague impressions can be very important when they are backed by the results of perceptual learning. They help to account for the fact that we seem able to take in so much more than three bits of information in a single perception, and also for the fact that our perceptions of organized wholes are often inaccurate and subject to sudden restructuring.

Electronic computing machines (electronic 'brains') work on two major principles. Digital computers handle precise information on the yes–no basis. They can represent any number in terms of a binary notation, using only the digits nought and one. In our decimal system of counting we have digits from nought to nine but above nine make our entries in terms of so many tens plus so many units, or so many tens of tens (hundreds) plus so many tens plus so many units, and so on. With the binary system we operate with multiples of two. We may have no units or one unit, no twos or one two, no fours (two twos) or one four. The number seven of our decimal scale would thus become 111 in the binary scale: one *four* plus one *two* plus one *unit*. A computer using this system gives answers accurate to any given degree.

Another type of electronic computer is known as an analogue computer. A simple analogy might be found in the use of a large graduated measure fitted with a tapped water supply and a tapped outlet. Such a gadget could be used to make additions and subtractions of numbers by the simple process of running in so many units of water for addition and running out so many for subtraction. All we should need to do would be to read the scale when the operations had been completed. By using electricity instead of water, and by making provision for several different types of operation to take place at the same time, complicated mathematical equations can be solved very simply.

Now the question arises as to which (if either) of these two principles applies to the working of our own brains. The answer appears to be that something of both is concerned. On the one hand we appear to have a coding system comparable to conversion into a binary scale. On the other hand we appear to have a matrix of tensions which result in a given position of equilibrium. This should be borne in mind while we are discussing perceptual learning.

WHOLES AND PARTS

The Gestalt psychologists have emphasized that any configuration (in the German, *gestalt*) is a whole having properties beyond those of any of its parts. So the tune is something more than the notes which compose it, and may even be the same tune when transposed into another set of notes. The words of Shakespeare's plays, when changed in their context, may be just a dictionary. In view of this it was argued that psychologists must study wholes and that to attempt to take a part is to destroy the very thing we wish to study. In a way this is true, but it overlooks the fact that part and whole are purely relative. The petal is part of the flower but it can also be regarded as a whole with its own parts. Again the flower is only a part of the plant, which again is just part of the garden.

The essential point here is that we have not only entities, but relations between entities whereby they can enter into larger wholes. Our universe appears to be constructed on a hierarchical principle: small things are parts of larger things, which again are parts of still larger things. Molecules of aluminium silicate constitute clay which, when shaped in a particular way and baked, becomes bricks, which again are put into certain relationships with other materials, to produce a house, a garden wall, or a factory, which, in turn, may be just parts of a town. This, of course, is a man-produced series, but the same principle applies to natural things, too, e.g. to our own bodies.

It should be noted that in this hierarchical development the nature of the part always places some restriction on the nature of the whole. If we build with bricks some forms which would be possible with steel are denied us, as, for example, modern skyscrapers. And if we build with bamboo and paper still other restrictions apply. Now, it is these very restrictions which give rise to many of our so-called laws; in fact, these restrictions are the laws. We must not digress to discuss this now, but we can emphasize that it is this hierarchical structure of the universe which makes possible the coding system by means of which we build up an efficient reference to make possible our perception of complex data.

FORMS OF PERCEPTUAL LEARNING

Object learning

The simplest of our perceptual units is what we might call an object. It would almost appear as if we just naturally see objects. As we look around we see not visual patterns of varying degrees of complexity as we might find in looking through wallpaper samples, but rather we see chairs and tables, cups and jugs, trees and people. Even when we view unusual objects they still appear to us as objects. How can we explain this tendency?

The figure–ground distinction which we have already mentioned is an important basis here. It leads us to focus on objects which have the property of being different from their background. We thus have repeated observations of the object, say a chair. Not all these observations are the same, however. In fact, we may never have two observations which are quite the same since the view varies with every change in our position. We may sometimes see two legs instead of four. Sometimes 'the square top may appear as a straight line, and its four sides will seldom, if ever, appear as of equal length owing to perspective effects. It appears, therefore, that we observe many different data. To our varying visual impressions are added impressions from other senses. In handling the chair we get tactile impressions of shape and hardness. We hear noises produced by varying contacts with the chair, as when something drops on it or when we bump it against the wall in carrying it. We experience its rigidity and support when sitting on it and so on.

How can we deal with all this confused data? How do we ever come to have a concept of a chair as a relatively unchanging object when our actual impressions of it are always varying? It is, in fact, the very variety of our impressions which really makes this possible. All these varying impressions are consistent with the chair being of a particular nature. The chair as we conceive it is the sort of object which would appear in these diverse ways under these varying conditions, and it is the very diversity of our impressions which confirms this. As one looks out from the city of Auckland one sees the island of Rangitoto, a long symmetrical outline rising to a crater peak in the middle. At least it appears long, but the interesting thing is that no matter from what position one views the island it still has the same shape, even when one sails past it, and gradually it dawns on one that the island is really circular. A similar process operates with our chair. We build up a mental construct, a notion of a chair with four similar-sized legs, a symmetrical seat, perhaps square, a back of certain thickness, and so on. This is a chair we have never seen and cannot possibly see. A child asked to draw the chair may make futile efforts to represent it in this way, putting in all the detail which he knows ought to be there, but the adult does not make such a mistake. He realizes that the chair must always appear in a particular aspect but he thinks of his mental construct as being the real chair.

It is a strange paradox that what we consider to be the actual chair is a mental construct, but there is no need for us to make a profound philosophical mystery of it. If we understand the nature of perception it is neither paradox nor mystery. The very notion of reality is conjured up in the same way as our notion of the chair, and it is all in aid of achieving drive satisfactions within the restrictions of our experience. We are concerned to code our experience in such a way that we may make use of it to further our satisfactions and the most efficient coding is the way which gives us the greatest insight into reality.

Map learning

This is concerned with the inter-relations of objects and probably developed first in terms of locomotion. We learn how to get to certain places such as food sources. Again we have the equivalent of a variety of viewpoints: a variety of starting-points. The route differs with the starting-point, but all routes are inter-related and can be explained in terms of a map. Our various locomotions within any area as motivated by our various drives (not excluding curiosity) lead us again to a construct such as can best be described as a map. It need not be a visual map, although for many people it will be. It may be a kinaesthetic or motor map. Some people have difficulty in picturing how a word may look when written and yet may have no difficulty in actually writing it. The pattern was stored away in what one might call a muscle memory rather than an eye memory. Such people may think of a place as being in a certain direction with a certain detour required to get to it. 'It is over that way; you go round the park and then down the river to the bridge, etc.' Another person sees a plan with the park, river, and roads appearing in more or less detail. But whatever the form the essential is something which can best be described as a map.

This point is well brought out by studies of maze learning. Much experimentation went on with this form of learning earlier in the century, and there was much discussion as to the nature of the learning. Some psychologists thought of it as the learning of a motor skill, a learning of what motor movements to make: six steps forward, turn to the right, etc., much as one would learn a dance. But actual experiments upset this idea. It was found that rats which had learned to run through a maze were quite capable of swimming through it when it was flooded. The fact that the previously learned running pattern was now in no way involved appeared to be little handicap. Depriving the rats of sight, smell, or hearing again failed to prevent their reaching the goal. The point was that they now 'knew' the maze. It was represented in their minds or brains by a cognitive map and, whatever the conditions, they could now adapt themselves and seek the goal accordingly. Note the essential similarity of such a map to the chair construct just described. Again it is the assumed form which will best fit all our experiences. It is a construct.

An interesting point arises here. Suppose some of the paths in the area of which we have the cognitive map are rough and difficult to travel over while others are quickly traversed. In our cognitive map the rough paths may appear as much longer than they would in a map strictly to scale. Nevertheless the cognitive map may be less misleading in actual use. This was brought home to the writer forcibly when he first lived in Wellington, which is a rather hilly city. He consulted a map and decided on the route to a house he had to visit. According to his map this was the shortest route, but he discovered part of his route was not a car road at all and he had to climb some hundreds of steps to get to his goal. There is something to be said for a map which is scaled in terms of hours instead of miles. The only difficulty arises when we have varied modes of transport, but at this stage our construct rises to the occasion and reconciles the divergent viewpoints.

Type learning

We have pointed out how the varied stimuli received from an object result in the formulation of a mental construct which is really our hypothesis as to the nature of the object which could cause us to have such experiences. We are here concerned with stimuli from the same object. Now we have to consider the case of similar objects. We referred to a particular chair, but there are many kinds of chairs, of different shapes and sizes and composed of different materials. What have all these in common, and to what extent can we usefully refer to them all by a single name? The answer to this question takes us a step further in our understanding of the cognitive coding system.

It would be difficult to decide from a consideration of diverse chairs what is common to them all. The kitchen chair may have four long and somewhat thin legs whereas the chesterfield may be totally devoid of legs and just rest on smooth metal plates. The seat may be four-sided or circular, padded or plain, sprung or unsprung. There are endless variations but all make some provision to support a person in a sitting position with some sort of backrest. This is something in common and probably basic to our idea of a chair. When we speak of a chair we refer to something which is capable of entering into certain relations and thereby having meaning for us.

A construct of this kind is known as a concept. It should be noted that concepts may occur at various levels. We may have a concept of a chair, but also a concept of furniture which includes chairs, tables, sideboards, etc. We may have a concept of dog, a wider concept of animal which includes horses and cats with dogs, a concept of vertebrates which includes all creatures with backbones (men, birds, and many fishes), and a still wider concept of living creatures. We shall go further into this in the next chapter on thinking, but it is important here to note that all this is involved in the hierarchical coding system.

The third dimension

We have already remarked that our seeing has to be mediated by a two-dimensional retinal pattern at the rear of the eye. How, then, do we come to see in three dimensions?

If the reader will glance round him for a moment he will realize that nothing appears more certain to him than that he perceives depth and distance. The explanation of this is again in the familiar terms of construct. The sensory pattern is full of cues which indicate the third dimension and we see what is in accord with these cues. Since all our perception depends upon the interpretation of sensory data in this way depth presents no special problem. Let us consider some of the cues involved:

1. *Retinal disparity*. Normally we see objects with two eyes and so receive two different views. The discrepancy between these two views varies according to our distance

from the object. Now, by our experience of moving our position, we already have evidence of distance and location, so we naturally bind our visual and motor experience into a common reference system so that a given retinal disparity *means* a certain distance. The importance of binocular vision in seeing in the third dimension is well brought out by the stereoscope in which we view two pictures of the same scene taken from slightly different angles. The effect is really startling. Various systems of movie projection have been developed to take advantage of the same principle, some with most impressive results.

2. *Focusing.* In order to see any object clearly we have to focus our eyes in the same way that it is necessary to focus a camera. By using a camera with an accurate focusing scale and adjusting the focus until the image appears with maximum clarity, it is possible to read off from the scale the distance at which the object is situated. In the same way we build up our own visual scales by means of which we can judge the distance of an object from the degree of muscular movement called for in our focusing muscles. At least, this appears very likely; there appears to be no conclusive evidence to establish it. It is also believed that the degree of convergence required to bring *both* eyes to focus on the same object provides a further clue. Just how important this may be is difficult to estimate since it becomes linked with the effects of retinal disparity. The fact that two photographs representing the two views normally available to the two eyes can produce varying distance effects while the eyes remain in a situation demanding no convergence (looking into the stereoscope) casts some doubt upon the importance of convergence. There is even some evidence that when we look at an object with one eye the other eye correspondingly focuses and converges. Perhaps all we can safely say is that within distances of a few feet eye adjustment does, in some form, provide clues as to distance.

3. *Interposition*. If one object is obscured partly by another it appears to be further away. This can be demonstrated by a neat experiment in which one playing card is stood up at some distance in front of another. It should appear nearer because it partially hides the more distant card. However, the observer is permitted to see the set-up only from a fixed peep-hole and part of the *nearer* card is cut away so that the whole of the distant card is now visible. The result is quite startling. The distant card now seems to be in front of the nearer card and partly covering it. Furthermore, the nearer card appears to be much larger than the distant card because it is seen as further away and, therefore, needs to be bigger in order to appear so big at this distance. By altering our cue we have thus misled the observer as to relative distance and relative size. This experiment provides an excellent example of how perception is organized according to the most likely interpretation of the various cues available and how the cues operate, not independently, but as a system.

4. *Size and perspective*. Distant objects appear smaller than near ones. If we know the actual size of an object we can judge its distance according to how small it appears to be. This is part of the general perspective effect. Railway lines seem to converge in the distance, lamp posts decrease in height, and so on.

5. *Aerial perspective*. Not only do distant objects appear smaller but also less distinct. This haziness produces a distinct impression of distance and is invariably applied by the artist. Obviously the state of the atmosphere will influence the clarity of view and must be allowed for. The story is told of a Londoner who visited Switzerland and set out to walk to a near-by mountain before lunch. At least it appeared near by by London standards, but the clear Swiss air had misled him so that with lunchtime approaching he was still far from his goal. At this stage he encountered a small

stream which he would normally have jumped without hesitation, but in view of his experience with the mountain he decided that he would have to remove shoes and socks to wade across! The latter part of the story is, of course, absurd but anyone who has experienced the startling differences produced by the unusual clarity of the atmosphere will appreciate the point of it.

6. *Light and shade effects*. The pattern of light and shade provides us with very important third-dimensional cues. This can be best appreciated by an actual example. The reader should try the effect of looking at the picture on this page with the book upside down.

Fig. 13.

7. *Movement of observer*. When we travel in a train and look out through the window we notice that objects close at hand are dashing past very rapidly but distant objects appear to move slowly, while the sun appears quite station-

ary. This differential rate of displacement when we change our viewpoint is constantly giving us cues to the relative relationships of objects in depth.

THE CONSTANCIES

As a man walks away into the distance the actual size of the image he forms on our retina decreases rapidly but we still tend to see him as of the same size. As we walk along the street we do not regard people on the other side as dwarfs but as normally-sized persons. The reader who has followed our argument so far will have little difficulty in understanding this situation. It is a question of the chair again. We formed a mental construct of what the real chair might be and changing apparent size was just one of the things which we had to account for. Having built up our construct of the chair we were no more confused by variations in apparent size than by variations in apparent shape. In fact, we have seen that knowledge of actual size provides us with clues as to distance. Our practical relations to the chair demand that we regard it as constant in size but we must take into consideration its distance from us. To attempt to sit on a chair which is too far away may produce unpleasant results.

Similar considerations apply to brightness effects. We see white paper as white, even though the amount of light reflected from it in the deepening twilight may be much less than normally reflected by black paper, and very much less than is reflected by black paper in bright sunlight when the black still appears black. It is customary to speak of this effect as 'brightness constancy' but it might be more meaningful to talk of 'object constancy'. The effect does, however, transcend particular objects, and it is convenient to talk of size and object constancies as permanent aspects of our perceptual activity. We develop the tendency to judge both size and brightness (or whiteness) in terms of the conditions obtaining. In the dim light we expect a white object to reflect less, and we make allowance in the same way as we do for an object at a known distance. If we look at the white object through a cylinder which cuts off all our view of other objects so that we have no reference frame to establish the general level of illumination, this allowance can no longer be made and the constancy effect disappears.

The value of the constancies in practical matters is easily apparent, and we must bear in mind that the human organism is adapted to deal with practical situations, i.e. with the satisfaction of drives. Our life consists of exploiting sensory cues for drive satisfaction. In this connexion we might refer to another perceptual problem which is sometimes raised. The visual pattern appears on the retina in inverted form as it does in the camera. Why do we not see the world upside down? The best answer might be that we do! What we really mean by upside down is that our visual cues are in reverse relationship to cues from other senses, so that we might reach up for something which is actually below us. A naïve view of perception would suggest the possibility of this, but it is not possible in terms of the theory of perceptual learning which we have been explaining. We must see things in a way which will fit in with all our experiences. This is confirmed by some interesting experiments carried out at Innsbruck, following up some earlier work by Stratton. Professor Erismann and Dr Kohler prepared special spectacles which have the property of inverting the image on the retina and had a man wear these for several weeks. When first fitted these produce a most disconcerting effect (as the writer can confirm from experience), and it is with extreme difficulty that one can walk down simple steps. At various stages in the experiment the subject was required to defend himself against sword thrusts with a shield. At first, when threatened in the lower part of his body he would raise the shield to the upper part, and vice versa. Next came a stage when he would reason, 'It looks as though I should move the shield down so I shall move it up', and, by conscious correction, could adjust his actions, although with great strain and very clumsily. Some days later he was able to carry out the appropriate actions with some skill. The world still appeared upside down, but he was able to make most ordinary movements with little difficulty. Finally came the stage when the world actually appeared the right way up again and he was completely adjusted. Now all his reference frames had become coordinated. At this stage he was able to ride a motor-cycle through the crowded streets of Innsbruck without being in any way inconvenienced by the inverting glasses.

THE INNATE BASIS OF PERCEPTION

The varied evidence of learning processes involved in the development of perceptual capacity could easily lead to the conclusion that all perception is dependent on learning. This is no more true than the older notion that we are miraculously endowed with full perceptual powers at birth. As with all psychological functioning the truth appears to be that we are innately provided with capacities which develop under certain conditions. We have already hinted, however, that some perceptual patterns may be capable of triggering certain responses prior to any learning: innate releaser patterns. There is evidence of something of this nature in relation to depth perception. Failure of the young organism to appreciate the danger of falling into holes or over cliffs could gravely menace its welfare and there is evidence that protection against this has developed.

Gibson and Walk carried out an ingenious experiment in which they supplied the visual appearance of a cliff but covered it with thick glass so that there was no actual danger. A baby refused to crawl over the edge of the cliff, but little could be concluded from this since by the time a baby can crawl it has already had much opportunity to learn from visual experience. Crucial evidence could be provided only by an animal capable of walking almost immediately after birth. For this purpose the goat was a suitable choice and it was found that little kids avoided the 'visual cliff' just as studiously as their human counterparts. Moreover, by suitable experiments, it was found that the clue for this response involved not a perspective effect but the focusing of the eyes. This may indicate that our first perception of depth is mediated by physiological clues and that the more subtle psychological factors are learned later.

In this matter of learning to perceive more effectively it should be emphasized that all the laws of learning are operative. In particular it should be remembered that those forms of perception which lead to drive satisfaction will be selected in just the same way as those motor activities which lead to drive satisfaction are also selected (operant conditioning).

This influence of drive satisfaction upon perception may lead to some paradoxical results. We may have 'wishful seeing' as well as wishful thinking. The famous 'Schafer faces' experiment illustrates this very neatly. Ambiguous profiles were presented to subjects in right and left facing forms. When one form was presented the subject was rewarded; when the other form was presented he was punished. When shown the ambiguous form without reward or punishment subjects reported 'seeing' the form that had previously been most usually rewarded. This experiment by Schafer and Murphy suggests that we can learn to perceive in a way that is not in accord with reality. Another experiment by Proshansky and Murphy confirms this. Subjects were asked to judge the length of lines. They were rewarded for reporting long lines and punished for reporting short lines. The result was a significant tendency to over-estimate length.

In actual practice the danger here considered is not important since, on the whole, rewards in real life depend upon veridical judgement. It would be most unusual for over-estimation of lines to be consistently rewarded except in the artificial conditions of an experiment. We perceive in the way that has been most effective in the past, and we have no other means of knowing what *is* veridical perception. Perception is but the means to drive satisfaction.

THE ACT OF PERCEPTION

We have now considered the framework in which perception takes place and the way in which we build up the reference frame which makes it possible. We shall now examine the factors which are operating in any particular case of perception.

1. We have the visual field structured in terms of various innate tendencies: figure–ground, proximity, similarity, and common movement.

2. Recognition takes place in terms of the coding system and the field is further structured in accord with this. Vague cues now suggest clear details because these cues are re-inforced by our expectancies.

3. Recognition itself consists of deciding between alternatives, and so is considerably influenced by *which* alternatives are presented first. The question of *set* thus becomes very important. If we have been telling ghost stories and then walk by a lonely churchyard in the dark, a moving white object will tend at once to be seen as a ghost. Whatever set is operating at the time will be important in determining the nature of our perception. Several factors may influence such set:

Familiarity

The relative efficiency of our coding reference for different areas is important. We perceive most easily those things with which we are most familiar. When he first uses a stethoscope the medical student is unaware of many sounds which later he will learn to recognize with little difficulty.

Recency

Coding patterns which we have just been using will be more readily available than others.

Drive

The operation of a strong drive will bias hypotheses in the direction of satisfying situations. The shipwrecked sailor will be alert to any suggestion of smoke from a passing steamer. The importance of drive is easily understood when one remembers that the whole system of cognitive reference has its justification in its value as a means to drive satisfaction.

Finally we may note that perceptual errors may arise because a wrong hypothesis has been accepted and that, because hypotheses towards which we are initially set are tried first, our errors are frequently in the direction of wishful thinking. Furthermore, we are less likely to doubt hypotheses which accord with our desires, while those which conflict may be tested very carefully in the hope that we shall find them unacceptable. This question will arise again in connexion with the topic of thinking, so we can leave it now.

An interesting experiment was carried out with 110 subjects with varying degrees of hunger deprivation (one to six hours). They were presented with photographs of five food objects and five non-food objects with exposures of one fifth of a second under varying degrees of illumination. It was found that subjects who had not eaten for three or four hours showed greater ability to recognize the food objects.

At six hours sensitivity was less, probably because the degree of hunger had actually decreased by this time. The experience of hunger is influenced by the usual eating rhythms, and when we get considerably past our usual meal time hunger is not so obvious.

12

THINKING

So far we have been concerned with the cognitive reference frame at the level of perception, the way in which the sensory input from the immediate situation becomes structured in terms of our coding systems. This structuring, however, is always relative to action of some kind and this, in turn, is designed to increase our affective satisfactions. Our primary aim is to maintain cognizance of our environment in such a way that we are always ready to take appropriate action in accord with our affects. We are in the position of an army headquarters receiving messages from various points and endeavouring to plot the minute-to-minute changes on its reference maps. Some orders will be issued almost automatically on receipt of a particular message. Others will arise out of a fuller consideration of the implications of the changed situation. Thinking corresponds to this last level of development, but if we are to understand it properly we must see it not as some new and mysterious process, but rather as an extension of the processes we have already studied at the perceptual level.

Motivation is always in terms of affective satisfaction, but this is possible only through adequate understanding of our universe. Understanding is thus the major means to achieve our goals, but it is also, via the curiosity drive, a goal in itself and an important source of affective satisfaction. It is small wonder that it pervades all our activity.

In perception we strive to structure the sensory output in terms of our coded data because in this way it becomes meaningful. We see houses or trees, wood or stone, squares or circles, aeroplanes or ships, etc. Only when it is thus structured do we feel *secure* and in a position to pursue drive satisfaction.

When conditions are unfamiliar we undertake active exploration to establish an adequate cognitive map. The unfamiliarity is experienced as a threat or a challenge. If we have been exposed to considerable danger it may figure largely as a threat against which we must seek adequate protection in terms of such further knowledge as we may acquire. But, if we have had frequent experience of adequately structuring unusual sensory inputs, we may regard the unfamiliar largely as opportunity for further similar satisfactions and will press on with the thrill of adventure.

In people of high intelligence and strong curiosity much time may be spent in the investigation of more complex relationships. The aim is to extend or simplify the cognitive reference frame, and this aim may be pursued deliberately without the challenge of unfamiliar stimuli. Such investigation will bring to light new relationships, such as that of germs to disease or of mosquitoes to malaria. Or, again, it may disclose a basic relationship which permits a more economical coding form, as in the discovery of the nature of atomic structure, or the law of gravitation. Much of this kind of activity depends not just on the structuring of sensory input but rather the manipulation of existing coding material.

MANIPULATION OF CODING

The universe is represented within our coding systems as constructs of various kinds, but not as a vast picture, rather as a Meccano set whose parts we can manipulate in various ways. We can reassemble these parts in a variety of ways and see what results. This ability to produce new combinations of our coding experience is usually referred to as imagination because it largely involves dealing with images. The word image is primarily related to our experience with mirrors and so usually has a visual reference. Many people have the ability to form a mental picture, not only of objects which they have previously seen, but objects of a kind which they have never seen: a spider with a man's face, a ship sailing on the land, a pig with wings, etc. Such imaginary objects are built out of constructs already available to us through our experience and we can imagine nothing which cannot be so constituted. The person blind from birth can never have a visual image of even an existing object such as a chair. He will certainly develop a construct corresponding to chair but it will lack the visual qualities, notably colour, which are found in the chair construct of the seeing person.

Although we tend to think primarily of visual material when we speak of images, we can also have images corresponding to all the other senses. So some people can hear auditory patterns mentally. They can think of a musical composition and actually 'hear' the music over again. Or they can look at a musical score, if they have learned to read music, and construct the melody in imagination. Others can experience muscular movements in imagination, or revive scents they have met before. People vary very much in the degree to which they can conjure up these various kinds of images, and, unless they have read books on psychology or given the matter considerable thought, tend to believe that other people have the same experience as themselves in this respect. It is difficult for a person who has vivid visual images to realize that there are some people who are practically devoid of such capacity.

It is often thought that people who are deficient in the one kind of imagery have correspondingly more of another kind, and it was once the custom to classify people as visiles, audiles, or motiles according to the predominant imagery. Unfortunately we know surprisingly little in this area, largely because imagery is such a private matter and no one can experience anyone else's, and there is just as much reason to believe that people who have good imagery of one kind have better-than-average imagery of another.

One reason why there has been so much neglect of imagery differences is that people seem to be able to behave intelligently despite such differences in imagery, and this is quite understandable since our coding system does not exist in picture form. We have a construct corresponding to *table* but it is not a particular view of a particular table. Many people will attach an image of a table to it and this may be a convenient label just as painting a chocolate on a chocolate box will tell us what is in it. It is just as effective, however, to use the word image as a label, and here one sensory modality is equivalent to another. In fact, for a concept it is more useful, since it is less misleading. A table image attached to our concept of table will be a particular colour, and many of the tables we wish to refer to under the concept will not be of this colour. Thinking at the concept level can proceed most efficiently when least fettered by concrete references, and this is why language provides such a convenient form for it.

Language consists essentially of a concept-level coding system. It provides us with an excellent system for coding above the perceptual level. The four words 'Man walked along road' provide us with an enormous amount of data. All that we know of man and all that we know of roads is involved in the reference. In picture form very much more detail would be called for, but most of this detail is probably quite unnecessary for our thinking reference and might obscure what we were concerned with rather than help. We must always bear in mind the limits to the moment-by-moment capacity of the mind. It cannot handle many independent bits of information at the same time, but there is no limit to the amount of information it can deal with if it is done up in sufficiently large parcels. *Road, man,* and *walk*, it can encompass quite easily as single concepts which the words distinguish, but, if we must concern ourselves with all the details of a particular road, we may spend hours on this alone.

We are anticipating too much here, so must return to the general question of coding manipulation. This can take place at all levels and may take place in several forms. The term 'thinking' is frequently used to designate most of them, so we shall have to consider them all and decide which we can include under this name.

TYPES OF CODING MANIPULATION

1. We may manipulate our coding material in order to work out the solution to a practical problem, the satisfaction of some drive. Instead of engaging in actual trial and check behaviour we carry out the trials mentally until we find what appears to be a workable plan which we then put into action.

2. We may play with our coding material in a more or less random fashion. One thing suggests another. We may see a thermometer on the wall which reminds us of another thermometer which we once bought, which in turn reminds us of the cold weather then experienced. This reminds us of the recent bad weather, of sun activity which has been asserted to be its cause, of atomic explosions which also produce heat, of the possibilities of space travel, and so on, *ad infinitum*. All this may appear to be random but it is still guided by affect. At each choice-point we choose the thing which most interests us, and we cannot continue this kind of activity long before some major motive has taken charge. If we are seriously concerned about anything it is astounding how any train of association seems to lead inevitably back to it. It is for this reason that this process of what is called 'free association' is used by psychiatrists who wish to

explore the more intimate and dominant motives of their patients.

3. Closely related to the above is the process of what we usually call 'day-dreaming'. The pattern here is clearer and more consistent. Again the process is guided towards a major need, particularly one which has been frustrated and denied normal satisfaction. As in the problem-solving situation described under 1, we build up a plan of action which leads up to the satisfaction of our frustrated drive. The important difference between the two approaches, however, is that in this case we do not limit ourselves to our known abilities or to likely possibilities.

We can imagine ourselves with unusual strength or unexpected abilities. We can marry a prince or inherit a fortune. We are limited only by our own imaginations. Our plan of action does not have to be one which is likely to succeed in practice because we are able to imagine the achievement of our goal as well as the means to its achievement. There are such wonderful possibilities in this solution of our problems that some people, unable to cope with the practical requirements of life, fall back completely on it. Unfortunately it fails to give physiological satisfaction with its psychological satisfaction (and even the latter is but a pale substitute), so that such people may require institutional care.

A small amount of day-dreaming, however, may be quite acceptable as a relief from the strain of living and may leave one stronger to face the daily stress. Many of us seek help in our day-dreaming from books and movies. We seek ready-made day-dreams. The gratification we get in this way may sometimes be less harmful than would attempts at realistic gratification. It is all a matter of reasonable balance.

4. The dreams which we have while asleep are closely related to day-dreams but involve some additional features which are not relevant to our present discussion, so we shall

merely mention them as another form of coding manipulation, even less free from restriction than our day-dreams.

5. The prime distinction between day-dreams and problem-solving is that the former is in no way bound by reality. At no stage do we have to submit our dream to reality testing, whereas our problem solution must always be tested in the fire of reality. There is an intermediate form of mental activity which in many respects resembles day-dreaming, but which has to face up to some reality testing in the form of social approval. Literary creations fall in this class. The wildest improbabilities may be incorporated, but the writer must always have an eye to his public. He must write of what they approve and in a form they approve. This form of activity may, therefore, present difficulties quite as great as does problem-solving, and some of its aspects may involve very similar situations. Both plot and form may present a series of actual problem-solving situations. It is for this reason that creative writing is frequently equated with creative thinking. From the psychological point of view there is an important difference. Furthermore, different abilities may be called for and the person who can succeed at one will not necessarily succeed at the other.

PROBLEM-SOLVING

We must now consider in more detail what is involved in problem-solving. The whole of living may be regarded as different aspects of problem-solving: the finding of appropriate responses to attain satisfaction. It is more convenient, however, to reserve this term for those situations where systematic efforts are being undertaken to obtain drive satisfaction. Such situations may be resolved in a variety of ways:

1. *Trial and check*. We have already noted that some aspects of learning might be described as problem-solving. The cat in the puzzle box is experiencing hunger and is

concerned to escape to food. Escape is the solution of the problem. Repeated escape produces learning but this is a secondary product.

The cat's activity in this situation is typical of problem-solving efforts when the situation is completely strange. Even an intelligent human being will resort to shaking the clock or tapping the radio, sometimes with effect. Such activity involves little that we might call thinking, but usually there is some dependence on our coded knowledge and the trials are seldom completely random. We may shake the clock but seldom try tracing figures of eight in the air above it!

2. Solution may be obtained in terms of the available coding. This may take place consciously or below the level of consciousness. At this stage, perhaps, we should discuss the meaning of the word 'conscious'. We have already referred to the limit on our perceptual input. There is probably just one aspect of the restriction on our attention capacity. It applies to the handling of 'imaginary' material just as much as to the sensory input, and it is the material which is thus being handled which we describe as being conscious. But the manipulation of our coding material is not limited to this conscious level. We know that there can be interactions without any conscious knowledge. For example, we forget a name and then, when we have given up the attempt to recall it, we find it suddenly popping up into consciousness. The nature of what has been going on in the meantime is by no means clear.

This unconscious cerebration plays a very important part in much of our problem-solving and has been designated *incubation*. The period of incubation may last days or weeks and during this period little may appear to be happening, but the idea of a possible solution may suddenly dawn on us, even when we are dreaming. Profound mathematical and scientific discoveries have been made in this way. The flash

173

of illumination or inspiration thus achieved may not supply the detailed solution if the problem is very complicated, but the result is just a matter of systematic work. It was in this way that the law of gravitation burst on Newton, and he was so overcome at first that he was unable to embark on the necessary mathematical calculations. Probably all original insights have appeared suddenly, in this way. It may be possible afterwards to justify them by a train of reasoning, but it would be impossible simply to reason one's way to the solution without the previous inspiration. It is easy enough to get to a place once you know just where you wish to go.

There is an important parallel between what happens in this sort of inspiration and what happens when a perception takes on meaningful structure. It is as if a search is going on in our minds to find the appropriate reference frame. What construct will reconcile these divergent impressions? Frequently the construct is just an extension of one already existing, as with Newton and the falling objects, and a chance coincidence points the application. In fact incubation may be largely a matter of keeping our problem as a continuing set which will finally make contact with an appropriate construct. This construct may be the result of perceptual experience, manipulation of data for other problem-solving, or the relatively random activation of constructs which occurs in dreams. Brilliant creative thought may thus be largely a matter of drive, of continuing affect, and this may explain why a person whose mental functioning appears to be at an unusually high level may yet never make any outstanding contribution, while a person who seems at times almost fumbling in his mental activity may solve a long-standing problem.

In the light of this discussion we may consider problem-solving as the evolving and testing of hypotheses. Where the problem is in a familiar area we may have an appropriate construct already available ready to supply at once the satisfactory hypothesis. Faced with a traffic blockage in a street we may at once form an hypothesis that a certain alternative route is probably open and have but to act on it. In other cases we must spend more time in searching for the solution; but whether we search by actual movement or resort to a mental review, the process is probably just a search, with all the luck of a search according to where we start first. The chief advantage of the mental search is that the material is all filed and cross-indexed, whereas the physical material is not so nicely arranged nor can it be searched without much physical effort.

3. Many of the problems with which we may be called to deal are just too complex for us to handle. What is required is not the answer but a set of answers, each of which constitutes a problem in itself. No search will find this set of answers in our coded experience since it does not exist. But if we can only break up our problem into a number of sub-problems and tackle them one at a time, we shall probably bring it within the range of our mental capacity. Thus, if we are faced with the problem of designing a calculating machine, our task is made manageable by first considering what are the different functions which we should look for in such a machine. Having decided on these we can proceed to a consideration of the way in which each could be served and how they might be integrated together. We find there are four basic arithmetical operations, addition being complementary to subtraction and multiplication complementary to division. Little insight is required to see the addition problem as essentially one of counting forward a given amount and to see that this can be easily accomplished by the use of gears so arranged that the first will move forward ten places and then push on the next gear one place. If now we have our gears registering numbers on two dials, one the number being added and the other the sum up to date, we have the solution for our addition problem. Subtraction

merely requires that we be able to work this operation in reverse so far as the total is concerned, but still in the same direction with regard to the registering of the number to be subtracted. This is a simple engineering problem.

At this stage we can take up the problem of multiplication and it may soon occur to us that this is only repeated addition. To find six times seven we have merely to add on seven six times. This again is a manageable engineering problem. And so we go on.

In the problem we have been considering our sub-problems turn out to be inter-related, but often this is not so. The problem of flying may be reduced to three sub-problems: a body of suitable structure for moving through the air, a light source of power, and suitable means of converting the power into propulsive energy. Each of these sub-problems may be further broken down into lower level problems. The question of the body may involve the finding of a suitable light yet strong material, the discovery of appropriate shape and so on.

The process of analysis which we have been describing is an essential one in much problem-solving. Many people fail to solve problems just because they have not developed the habit of making such analysis, and there is no doubt that training and practice can be very important in this respect. The analysis itself does, however, make great demands on insight and may be the major difficulty in achieving the solution of problems. This brings us to the further point that problems often remain unsolved because they have not been suitably defined. Sometimes we do not even get to the stage of seeing what a problem really is. The monkey which vainly strives to jump high enough to reach the bananas suspended from the ceiling is failing with his problem. When he sees it is essentially too great a distance between the floor and the bananas he may hit upon the idea of piling boxes on the floor and then climbing on them.

4. We have said that problem-solving requires the manipulation of our coding material. We have also made it clear that our coding material is organized in a hierarchical fashion and may be manipulated at various levels. We may work with concrete images of chairs and tables or we may use words of varying degrees of abstractness. Now it is interesting to notice that a problem which appears in one form of coding material may be translated into terms of another, and so become much easier to solve. Suppose a boy is faced with the problem of finding a half of 37⅜. By drawing a line of corresponding length and folding the paper he can get the answer by simple measurement.

Many problems can be reduced to the symbols of algebra, which can then be manipulated according to mathematical rules. While this manipulation is going on the meaning of the symbols in terms of the problem concerned may be completely forgotten. When the solution has been obtained the symbols are translated back into the language of our original problem. This case is not different in principle from the paper-folding example cited above.

INDIVIDUAL DIFFERENCES

13

COGNITIVE DIFFERENCES

INDIVIDUAL DIFFERENCES

THE discussion of thinking naturally leads to the question of intelligence and individual differences in thinking capacity. This in turn raises the question of individual differences generally. It is interesting to note that this is a psychological interest of quite recent development. Earlier psychologists were concerned about the basic principles, but since these applied to all people they did not find any cause to ask how people differed from one another. The problem of vocational guidance and selection fostered the new interest, but it began in connexion with education. Teachers had long found that some children made very slow progress in their studies and explained this in terms of deficient capacity. For the school administrator this was too facile an explanation. For him poor academic performance could also be attributed to inefficient teaching and it became of some importance for him to be able to decide, in any particular case of inferior school performance, whether the cause lay chiefly in the individual or in the instruction.

It was this educational problem which led to the first effective tests of intelligence. Alfred Binet and Th. Simon were assigned the task of producing an intelligence test which would enable the detection of defective children and so provide an answer to the teachers who complained that they were called upon to teach ineducable children. This was in France in 1904. Sir Francis Galton in England had evolved a number of tests in connexion with his interest in human heredity and must certainly be regarded as one of the most important pioneers in the development of mental testing. James McKeen Cattell in the U.S.A., who was also the author of several tests, was the first to use the actual term 'mental test' but it was with the work of Binet and Simon that the movement really got under way.

The essence of the Binet approach was the asking of a variety of questions which could be answered at different stages of development. In this way it was possible to get a measure of mental age. This was very suitable for the problem with which he was faced, since a boy with a mental age of only five could not be expected to keep pace with his fellows who had a mental age of nine or more. Instead of setting their expectations according to the chronological age of their pupils teachers were able to face the matter more realistically in terms of mental age. For some purposes, however, this was not so satisfactory. If one wished to compare the intelligence of a child of five and a child of nine one had to consider more than mental age. The nine-year-old might have the greater mental age and yet be, in a very real sense, the less intelligent child in that his mental age was less than average for his age, while that of the five-year-old might be greater than average for his age.

The need to be able to compare children of different ages with due allowance for their chronological age led Stern, a German psychologist, to suggest the *Intelligence Quotient* or I.Q. which is simply mental age divided by chronological age and multiplied by 100 in order to avoid fractions. Where the two ages are the same the I.Q. thus comes out at 100. Where mental age is higher the I.Q. exceeds 100. About half the population have I.Q.s which fall between 90 and 110 and only one person in a hundred has an I.Q. above 140 with modern tests. On the other hand about three people in a hundred will have I.Q.s below 70, with varying degrees of feeble-mindedness. (It should be noted that some of the earlier tests used a different basis and gave a greater spread of I.Q.)

THE NATURE OF INTELLIGENCE

So far we have taken it for granted that we know what we mean by intelligence. Unfortunately psychologists have been by no means agreed on this. Binet took a very practical approach. He assumed that intelligence develops with age and set about finding questions which could be answered by the average child at the various school ages. His test, which has been revised several times, still operates on this principle. The child is asked to distinguish coins, name a chair, distinguish objects in pictures, explain what makes a sailing boat move, give reasons why children should not be noisy in school, repeat digits backwards, find the absurdity in a picture or statement, solve problems, and so on.

Now we can certainly assume that intelligence will increase during the early years of development and therefore that the items which make greater demands on intelligence will not be within the capacity of younger children. It does not follow that the reverse is also true: that questions which can be answered only by older children must measure intelligence. Other things besides intelligence develop with age. Height, speed of running, and other physical attributes also develop with age but are not necessarily indicative of intelligence. We need a more satisfactory way of ascertaining which items measure intelligence.

Spearman suggested a mathematical approach. This was based on the technique of correlation which enables us to take the scores made by a group of people on two tests or examinations and state in numerical terms the degree to which the two tests agree in their results. If the scores from one test are perfectly consistent with those of the other so that the person who came first in one would also come first in the other and similarly for the second, third, and other persons, the lowest person having the lowest scores in both tests, the correlation coefficient would come to 1·00. If the tests gave completely opposite results so that the person who was the top in one came bottom in the other, the correlation coefficient would be − 1·00, while if there were no consistency at all, as would happen if we assessed the scores by taking numbers out of a hat, the correlation would be zero.

If we take a number of tests alleged to measure intelligence and calculate the correlation of each test with all the others we should get an appreciable correlation in each case. If we don't we can conclude that the two sets are not measuring the same thing and therefore one at least is not a measure of intelligence. Spearman investigated many tests in this way and found that even tests which were not supposed to be intelligence tests did correlate one with another and also with tests which were supposed to be tests of intelligence. He concluded that some sort of ability enters into all test performance and proposed that this common ability be more precisely defined and substituted for the concept of intelligence. To avoid confusion he proposed to refer to this common factor in test performance as 'g', really an abreviation for 'general intelligence' but not committed to any lay interpretation of the term.

At first Spearman was inclined to explain all differences in test results in terms of variation of 'g' capacity, and writers who refer to him frequently overlook the fact that he later agreed that there are many *group factors* (this term is used because of the mathematical analysis but it here means ability or capacity). The difference between these group factors and the general factor 'g' was that they influenced the results of some tests but not all, whereas 'g' had some effect on all test results. He compared the special abilities to engines and 'g' to the power which operated them. Special efficiency in one engine would not make for better functioning of another engine, whereas better 'g' would improve the performance of all our engines. The analogy explains his point very well, but we must not take it too seriously nor its implication. So far we have found no neurological equivalents for power or engine, and even the psychological significance of Spearman's theory has been seriously questioned.

Until only a few years ago American and British writers were in disagreement as to the existence of 'g'. The usual American approach found group abilities but no 'g', while the British methods always found 'g'. Fuller understanding of the mathematical methods of *factor analysis*, as the more advanced work with these correlation techniques is called, has shown that the British methods exaggerated 'g' effect while the usual American approach obscured it. We are now all agreed that there is a 'g' manifested in most tests. The chief question is as to the explanation of 'g'. It has been suggested that the general ability can be explained in three major ways.

The first of these involves all-round development of many abilities, average high ability. Some people are fortunate in being well endowed in many ways. It is often said that one cannot have brains and beauty too, but careful measurement shows that this is not true. On the whole, intelligent people have more than their share of good looks. Anyone who doubts this should look at photographs of mental defectives. But if people who are well endowed in one respect are also well endowed in many others we shall necessarily get the same effect as from a general factor. If the man with an expensive car has also an expensive lawn mower, a super refrigerator, and a high-powered radio he will get high general performance in just the same way as if he had average machines but a superior form of power to use in them. This source of general factor effect may be distinguished as *concomitant endowment* and is a general factor at the genetic or inheritance level rather than at the psychological level.

Secondly, we may get a general factor effect from what has been called *vicarious functioning* or the carrying out of the function of one ability by another. Thus a blind man can walk around avoiding obstacles by noting the difference in sound produced by the tapping of his stick when an obstacle is close. In this respect he uses his ears to replace his eyes. Many psychological abilities can switch over in this way, and this too enables us to keep a high level of performance.

Thirdly, we have a true general factor at the psychological level, that is an ability which is able to boost up performance in a wide variety of tasks. It is this which best conforms to common ideas of intelligence. Of all the abilities this has the greatest capacity for vicarious functioning. In this way it can improve all kinds of activities. The schoolboy, who had to write out a word several hundred times and strapped several pencils together so that he could write several words at once, provided an excellent example of this. In fact there are few tasks the performance of which is not improved by some intelligent planning. It is here that we have the basis for the concept of intelligence. It is really capacity for problem-solving, but it should be remembered that even problem-solving may be influenced by a number of factors. We shall discuss these group factors and then return to a further consideration of 'g'.

It should be clearly understood that, in describing three different sources of 'g' effect, we are not suggesting three different forms of intelligence. We are simply explaining the effects which appear when we attempt to measure intelligence. Vicarious functioning is to be regarded as an interfering influence in our testing and one whose effect we would wish to eliminate. Concomitant endowment is also an interfering influence in that it makes it difficult to distinguish between high average ability and great insight capacity. Obviously there is a considerable difference between having a high performance level with regard to many specific abilities and having a considerable capacity for insight. It is the latter which would most correspond with the public understanding of what is meant by 'intelligence'. We would argue that this is the sense in which we should use the word and that high average ability (concomitant endowment) should be recorded by specific measures of the particular abilities or aptitudes involved. This will be better appreciated after a consideration of the primary aptitudes which are measured by the group factors.

GROUP FACTORS

The name of Thurstone is outstanding in this area. He and Mrs Thurstone (also a psychologist) reported the basic work which established the existence of at least seven group factors. Other workers confirmed the group factors and recent large-scale investigations leave little doubt about the matter. The chief difficulty is that more and more group factors of less and less importance are being discovered. From the practical point of view many of these can just be ignored. From the theoretical point of view what is needed is some further insight into the structure, particularly the neurological structure underlying these small factors. We shall concern ourselves here only with well established factors which are likely to be of sufficient importance to be taken into consideration in relation to vocational choice.

VERBAL ABILITY

It has long been noticed that people differ very much in their capacity to handle words and this is not necessarily related to their intelligence. Proverbially we speak of 'the gift of the gab', but while a person so gifted is hardly likely to be a mental defective he may have rather less intelligence than a person who lacks his ability to marshal words. In fact the flow of words may well obscure deeper thinking. Of a certain person it was said, 'She put her brain into neutral and let her tongue idle on!'

This verbal ability seems to involve two distinct factors: one concerned with the grasping of ideas and word meanings and the other concerned with fluency in dealing with single and isolated words. The first is denoted 'V' and the second 'W'. The former may be measured by the extent of vocabulary while the latter is indicated by the ability to think of many words of a specific kind in a short period, e.g. names of objects or words beginning with a particular letter. It is the first of these abilities which plays a leading role in many of our activities. Since many of our problems have to be expressed in verbal terms and as much of our thinking is expressed in the verbal form of coding material, lack of facility with words may gravely handicap the 'g' functioning. An analogy may be useful here. We think of a car driver as being good or bad as the result of his natural aptitude and training, but his actual performance on any given occasion will also depend on the nature of the car he is driving. Give him an old crock with poor acceleration and faulty brakes and he will certainly not make the showing possible in a high-powered recent model. Similarly the person poorly equipped with verbal aptitude may have his problem-solving performance handicapped.

SPATIAL ABILITY

This is probably the second of the group factors in order of importance. It provides us with another major vehicle for our thinking. Probably these two factors represent the two major coding systems: direct coding in terms of visual, tactile, and motor experience and indirect coding in terms of words. As in the case of verbal ability we find that high spatial ability has an important effect upon specific forms of problem-solving. This has been recognized by the construction of intelligence tests in verbal and 'non-verbal' form. The latter usually make use of some pictorial representation. Fig. 14 would be typical of this kind of test. One is asked to choose from several alternatives the appropriate content for the fourth square. The reader will have little trouble in deciding what is required here, even without the help of items from which to choose, but more complicated examples may pose a really difficult problem.

Fig. 14.

Now, although such a test and a verbal form of intelligence test usually give somewhat similar results, there are sometimes startling discrepancies, so that a person who is among the top five per cent in one is below average in the other. This is another case of the car and the driver.

The example just given is of an intelligence test in spatial form. Tests designed specifically to measure spatial ability permit of as little reasoning as possible. Typically one is required to choose one of several diagrams to fit a shown gap in another. The question may be made more difficult by requiring two parts to be fitted together in order to form the gap.

Ability of this kind is assumed to be of advantage in certain occupations such as engineering and architecture, but just how important is still open to doubt, as the possibility of vicarious functioning often queers the results. It is interesting to note, however, that Swineford found a correlation of ·78 between spatial ability and success on mechanical drawing, while the correlation with success in English was − ·08. English, on the other hand, correlated ·39 with verbal ability and mechanical drawing − ·47 with verbal ability.

PERCEPTUAL SPEED

This factor gets its name because it is manifested in the speed with which easy perceptual material can be handled. One form of the tests used requires one to compare many pairs of six digit numbers and note whether they are the same or different. Letters may be substituted for numbers to avoid complications with people who have an aversion for numbers. Such tasks seem to be related to the span of attention, which we mentioned in our discussion of perception, and it seems that we may have here a widespread factor which will enter into a number of tasks which require quick responses, e.g. controlling a motor-car or aeroplane, carrying out routine clerical work. Speed of problem-solving may be expected to be influenced when many hypotheses have to be tried, but where insight in terms of known principles is involved it may have little importance.

NUMERICAL ABILITY

All tests involving number have something in common which has been designated the N-factor. This is not a mathematical factor and it is not important with the more complex arithmetical operations. It is at its maximum in simple operations like subtraction and multiplication. As a vocational predictor it probably has little importance except for low-grade clerical work. In one investigation it had a correlation of − ·32 with success in general science, the reverse of what one would expect. It is likely that we have still much to learn about the true nature of this factor. It may even turn out that it is largely due to the early formation of negative attitudes to number material because of unpleasant experiences at school. There is no doubt that many people do have an aversion to anything which savours of arithmetic and that their school experience in these cases has usually been unpleasant. Moreover, this aversion seems to influence their handling of numbers in other than arithmetical ways, e.g. when called upon to memorize a number. All this might be explained in terms of a real lack of aptitude which had led to a neglect of numerical material.

MEMORY

This is a commonsense concept as well known as intelligence but it has caused much trouble to psychologists. For some time it was asserted that we should speak of memories rather than of memory since the ability to remember seemed to be specific to the material concerned. A man who could not remember the registration number of his own car might be able to tell you how many runs were made in the first cricket Test twenty years ago. The artist who had just painted a picture from memory might be unable to remember where he had left his umbrella. It all seems very confusing but some order is coming out of it all.

The present position appears to be that we can postulate three factors concerned with what is normally thought of as memory. One of these is *span memory*, which has more relation to perceptual speed than to the other two memory factors. It is simply a measure of how much one can retain of unrelated material (such as numbers or letters) after one presentation.

We have already pointed out that the limitations on this capacity are of the three-bit order which we find in perceptual activity and which we might expect to underlie perceptual speed. Memory-span and perceptual speed, however, are not identical, probably because some further influence is also involved in the latter.

The second form of memory is *rote memory*, which again involves unconnected material such as lists of words or syllables, but involves a time period of minutes rather than seconds. Related to this is the third form of memory, that for *meaningful* material. The reason why this comes out as a separate factor is doubtless because it depends to a considerable degree on meaning, which again depends on understanding, and the availability of suitable coding material. Some tests which might be expected to involve chiefly this factor, e.g. remembering a paragraph with considerable detail so as to be able to answer specific questions about the content, turn out to involve chiefly the verbal factor. All things considered, therefore, it looks as though we can consider rote memory to be the key to the memory group.

FLUENCY

Irrespective of the actual range of vocabulary, people vary very much in the speed with which they can mobilize words. If asked to produce during one minute as many words as possible beginning with a given letter or related to a given theme some persons can proceed with little hesitation while others will repeatedly stall. This verbal fluency is among the best-attested of the group factors. It is sometimes referred to as F (for fluency) and sometimes as W (for words). As already noted, this is not to be confused with the verbal factor (V) which is more a matter of extent of vocabulary and actual understanding of concepts. It has little relation to intelligence but can be of considerable importance in many practical spheres and in relation to some occupations.

OTHER FACTORS

There are several factors concerned with various aspects of reasoning and problem-solving (induction and deduction, hypothesis verification, perception of abstract similarities, and flexibility) which, from a practical point of view, may in the meantime be considered as special aspects of 'g'. Factor analysis is an excellent means of isolating functional units, but unless these units can be incorporated meaningfully into a psychological schema we must be cautious about unduly multiplying our concepts. Furthermore there are many factors which can be distinguished mathematically by studying a group of people, but which cannot be measured in anything like pure form in a single individual. At the physiological level we may be able to demonstrate that the thickness of a person's skin influences his weight, but if we have to depend on gross weight as the only indication of skin thickness this does not help us very much. This is just an exaggeration of the position we find ourselves in with regard to some of the minor psychological factors.

There are several other ability factors which have been found of practical importance. *Reaction time* and *motor co-ordination* are useful predictors of pilot success. Several abilities, such as pitch discrimination, are essential for musical success although not, in themselves, sufficient to ensure it. A variety of more or less specific factors enter into drawing and similar artistic abilities.

ABILITIES AND APTITUDES

These two words are used rather loosely in much psychological literature but there is general agreement that 'ability' refers to the current level of achievement whereas 'aptitude' always has some predictive reference. The former term has the wider meaning since we can measure an aptitude only in terms of current performance. We have therefore used the term ability in referring to factors so as always to play safe. In many cases, however, we should have preferred to use the term aptitude because it is in this sense that the factor is chiefly important.

The term aptitude itself is used in two very different ways. In one case we mean a basic innate capacity. So we might talk of verbal aptitude or spatial aptitude. In the other case we are concerned with general suitability for some particular occupation as when we talk of clerical aptitude or engineering aptitude. Here many primary aptitudes may be concerned together with the results of training. Thus perceptual speed and knowledge of spelling may both be important components of clerical aptitude. To avoid confusion as between these two usages of 'aptitude' it is desirable always to use an adjective and to speak of *primary aptitudes* or *occupational aptitudes*. The former will be largely innate and even the latter are usually thought of as depending predominantly on innate capacities. Unfortunately we have no sure means of measuring the innate element in aptitude. We strive in our tests to differentiate between the current achievement level and the potential for development but we can do this only indirectly. An intelligence test may be a better predictor of future success in the study of history than would a measure of present historical knowledge, but the intelligence test itself depends upon current level of achievement.

HEREDITY AND ENVIRONMENT

We may usefully pause here to ask what value there is in the concept of innate aptitudes. The fact that we can never obtain a direct measure of such innate aptitude need not prevent its being a useful concept. So far no one has been over the sun with a tape measure, but we find it quite useful to conceive of the sun having size. Unfortunately the role of heredity in psychology has often been wrongly conceived. The question can never be: is this due to heredity or environment? Rather we should say: to what extent do heredity or environmental factors influence this rate of development?

There can be no doubt that, without suitable environment, no satisfactory development can take place, but it is also true that without satisfactory heredity there is an equal impossibility of development. The young bird which is starved to death will never fly, but all the food in the world will not make a dog fly. No baby which is denied the contact of other human beings can ever manifest more than primitive intelligence, but also there are feeble-minded individuals for whom no environment could ever develop their intelligence to average level. A useful comparison is with a farm. A farm in a rich river valley with a warm climate and adequate rainfall will require little cultivation to make it respond with heavy crops. But a farm in arid hilly country with a poor rainfall will make little return without much cultivation and, although further improvements in cultivation will always bring some increment in return, the stage is soon reached when the cost of improving cultivation is out of all proportion to the small increase in returns. In fact the additional cultivation would bring far better results if bestowed on the fertile farm which already has rich crops!

The situation with human beings is parallel to this. And just as it is useful to assess the natural fertility of a farm (although this can never be done precisely) so it is useful to assess the natural aptitude of a human being. The fertility of the farm might be assessed in terms of the gross return for a given expenditure per acre of cultivation. The relative importance of natural fertility and cultivation at any particular stage of development might then be assessed by asking: what increase in return will I get if I increase my expenditure on cultivation by £x? If the answer is 'practically none' then I may assume that, at this stage, natural fertility is almost one hundred per cent important.

Similar concepts may be applied to human ability. The question we usefully ask is: with the present degree of education and learning opportunity what are the relative influences of heredity and environment in determining the level of functioning? The answer to such a question is meaningful only in relation to the present level of development. With more or less opportunity for learning the answer would be different. But it is a useful answer because it tells us something about the present situation and enables us to make some guess as to what the position might be with a little more or a little less opportunity for learning.

We are only just beginning to ask intelligent questions of this kind with regard to human aptitudes and traits and so far we have only tentative answers for 'g' and one or two major traits. For 'g' the answer appears to be that heredity accounts for 75 to 80 per cent of the variation in ability. In this sense heredity is more important than education for intelligent behaviour.

14

AFFECTIVE DIFFERENCES

In the last chapter we have been concerned with individual differences as they affect the means system. We have now to consider the major differences between one individual and another on the motivational side. Here it may be argued that each individual has a unique affective reference frame and that only a detailed knowledge of this will be useful in understanding his motivation. In a sense this is true, but we have seen that all our perceiving and understanding depends upon suitable coding of our experiences in the form of concepts. This certainly applies here and any understanding of personality differences must depend upon the development of concepts at various levels. The complete description of any personality would probably require much longer than the lifetime of the individual concerned, but we may be able to convey much about its major aspects in a few minutes *provided we have the appropriate constructs available in our coding* just as we are able to perceive considerable detail in a scene in a few seconds if we have the necessary cognitive reference frame.

Our discussion of the affective reference frame suggests that we might look for the major differences between individuals at the level of drive, trait, sentiment, or self-ideal. Factor analysis of various personality measures has found factors which can be conveniently ordered in this way. Clinical experience and common-sense observation confirm many of these findings. Systematic factorial research has still much to do and the wealth of studies now being reported is bringing to light many factors which still have to be confirmed and fitted into a consistent schema of psychological knowledge, but already a definite picture is beginning to emerge. We set this out as follows:

Differences at drive level

1. General: *General emotionality*.
2. Specific: Probably all drives but, in particular, *timidity* (fear), *assertion* (anger), and *kindliness*.

Differences at trait level

Outstanding differences here are to be found with regard to such traits as:
sociability
dominance
introversion
anxiety
nervous tension
suspiciousness

Differences at the level of the self-ideal

obsessional tendency
ego-drive
ego-control
euphoria, surgency, and rhathymia

Differences at the level of sentiment

The major individual differences here come under the classification of *interests*.

DIFFERENCES AT DRIVE LEVEL

The general affective factor

The history of emotional factors has been very similar to that of cognitive factors. We have the same early claims for a general factor and the same opposing claim for multiple group factors without a general factor. The chief difference is that the opposing claims have not yet been completely reconciled although there is every indication that the same type of solution will apply.

Webb (1915) produced the first evidence of a general factor which he called 'W' (for will, not for Webb). He used an early form of factor analysis and there is no doubt that his general factor was influenced by several things, notably by what is called *halo effect* in the ratings. This is such a common occurrence in psychological measurement that it merits some explanation. If anyone is asked to rate a person, whom he knows sufficiently well, on a number of personality variables, he will tend, in the case of each separate variable, to be influenced by his general opinion of the person. If he has a high opinion of the person he will tend to rate him high on all desirable qualities and low on all undesirable qualities and vice versa if he has a low opinion. The less certain he is about any particular quality the more he will be influenced by this halo effect. Whenever one person rates a number of persons this halo effect is likely to be present and will result in a general factor in the analysis.

Although this halo effect was important in producing Webb's 'W', further analyses of the same material by more recent methods and by several different people have shown that there is something more present. This was confirmed by Burt (1915), who was working on this problem at the same time as Webb. Burt called his general factor *general emotionality* and saw it as a parallel to the cognitive 'g'. This 'E', as it was dubbed, appeared to be simply the inverse of 'W', but its nature, thanks to Burt's better method, was much clearer. It appeared to involve a general tendency to emotional instability. The person with high 'W' remained stable and dependable under extreme stress. The person with high 'E' became emotional and lost his head with very little provocation.

Since this early work numerous researches have brought this factor to light in various forms. No other factor is so widely confirmed. Eysenck studied neuroticism and found a major factor underlying it. This factor appears to be the same basic factor. Some English work suggests that the factor primarily affects fear and anger responses and, as these are related to autonomic activity, it seems possible that this general factor may be one concerned with sensitivity of the autonomic system and would correspond to what we called *excitement* in our discussion of drives. It does not necessarily involve either anger or fear but does involve some degree of feedback from the autonomic nervous system.

Recent neurological findings seem to be related to this mechanism. Nerve currents in passing through the lower brain appear to bring about a general stimulation of the core of the lower brain and this spreads to the similar part of the mid-brain. This area is known as the *brain stem reticular system* and its activity is correlated with the arousal of attention. It is stimulated, however, not only by sensory input but by *descending* impulses from the cortex (outside layer of the upper brain) and by autonomic activity. This system is closely related to the *thalamic reticular system* which has a number of more specific connexions to other brain centres.* It seems to throw some light on the nature of sleep, attention, and emotion. Its function appears to relate to evaluating sensory input in terms of its relevance for the organism and so mediating high or low degrees of emotional involvement in the situation. Whether

* On page 85 we referred to neurological changes related to the direction of attention. The reticular system is probably concerned with this directing process. It would appear that the brain does not just receive sensory impulses but is able to monitor its own input. The specific control of sensory input is probably related to the *drive* mechanisms. The temperament factor which we are considering here is concerned with the sensitivity of this attention system.

the garrison shall sleep with only a guard on duty or whether the whole should be in a turmoil of activity may depend upon the state of this reticular and related systems.

The relation between emotion and sleep tendencies has always been recognized by common sense. We know that sleep is not dependent upon the amount of fatigue but that it will elude us when we feel quite worn out. We know that nothing is so destructive of sleep as fear, anger, or the state we have here described as excitement. We know that sensory stimuli tend to arouse us from sleep and that, in the absence of sensory input or with monotony of sensory stimulus (which really amount to the same thing since it is only change which can be meaningful), we tend to become drowsy and go to sleep. It is quite reasonable to suppose, therefore, that people might differ in the degree to which they respond to this arousal mechanism. One might almost suggest that it is concerned to assign personal significance to sensory input so that the activities of the organism as a whole may be adjusted, almost as a guard might be instructed to ring a bell once for a minor threat but to ring several times if the danger were really great. Under these circumstances guards might differ considerably in the scale they used to measure danger. So, with people, some tend to become totally involved in a situation much more than others. For them even trifles may be highly important and involve considerable autonomic activity.

It is easily understandable that people who are very sensitive in this way are more likely to break down under the stress of living and become neurotic since both psychologically and physiologically they are experiencing more stress, but, similarly, it must be understood that such people are, by virtue of their greater sensitivity to significance, capable of psychological and aesthetic insights denied to those less endowed in this way. To think of such a factor as *neuroticism* is highly misleading except in a pathological context. A rare violin is much more fragile than a tin whistle, but to describe its superiority in terms of fragility would be to miss the point unless we were concerned with the instruments solely from the point of view of transport.

The precise nature of this emotionality factor has still to be worked out. Before long it may be possible to relate it to specific features of the structure and function of the neurological and humoral systems, but even now it seems sufficiently well established that a factor of broadly the nature we have described does exist and that it has obvious neurological correlates.

Differences in specific drives

It is probable that individuals differ in the relative strength of all the drives. Some of these, such as differences in hunger, may not have great practical importance, while others are likely to influence a wide area of behaviour. The importance of such differences will vary from one culture to another. In a primitive society hunger variations might be very important, whereas in the 'welfare state' they may matter little. Our knowledge of major personality differences has been obtained largely by factor analysis of various measures of behaviour tendency, chiefly in the form of answers to questionnaires. The findings are thus restricted to the conditions of Western society and by the limitations of the techniques used. Some evidence of a factor concerned with variations in strength of the sex drive has been found. We know from research such as that of Kinsey that pronounced differences do exist with regard to this drive, and it seems likely that such differences will have an important bearing on behaviour. Investigators in this area, however, confront special difficulties.

No factor based on curiosity seems to have been established although one might expect that variations in the strength of this drive might be of considerable significance in a scientific age. The explanation appears to be that this drive exerts its influence chiefly in the area of interests where it plays a very important part. Three major personality factors seem to be related directly to drive strength:

1. *Timidity.* Burt's research, to which we have already referred, found as the second most important factor one which contrasted the shy, socially-timid person with the assured, confident one who enters easily into social relations. Eysenck, in his studies of neurotics, has recently found a factor which distinguishes dysthymics from hysterics and which seems to involve a similar contrast. The dysthymics are characterized by anxiety, which might be conjectured to be related to an undue strength of the fear drive.

The factor is very well attested. In one form or another it turns up in all researches where appropriate measures are included. In a factor analysis involving many variables we usually find factors such as sociability, social dominance, and self-confidence, but these are correlated factors united by a 'second-order' factor. Such a second-order factor could be the result either of the primary factors producing certain effects in common, or of the primary factors being themselves partly the product of an underlying more basic factor due to inherited differences. It is most probable that in this case both explanations are involved to some degree, but recent research by Cattell indicates that heredity may be the more important.*

It is easy to see how timidity can retard the seeking of social contacts. The timid person may find support in the presence of a friend or in discussing his problem with a single friend, but a number of people who are not so well known to him arouse his anxiety since he is not sure whether he can cope with them. He knows that his timidity makes him appear in a poor light and so he is in a vicious circle,

* *American Journal of Human Genetics,* 1955, 7, pp. 122–46.

made more afraid because of his very fear. In fact his fear may be a greater problem to him in a social situation than in facing physical danger, since in the former case he feels he is being judged and found wanting. This attitude of timidity is evident in the very early years of a child's life. There is rapid conditioning to any threatening stimulus, diffidence in approaching strangers, sensitivity to rebuke and little tendency to dominate other children. Such children may show violent anger against *things* but when angered by another person they will tend to sulk rather than be aggressive and generally their anger will yield priority to fear.

Despite the importance of such an hereditary bias towards fear, it has to be remembered that environmental influences may often play a crucial part. Exposure to many fear stimuli will weaken the confidence of even a bold person. A weak physique may place a child at such a disadvantage in the struggle with his peers that he learns always to give deference to them, and bullying may well develop timidity in a person with little original bias in this direction. Conversely, the child who finds that he is able to get his own way by bullying others has this behaviour reinforced and may become aggressive although naturally of a somewhat timid disposition. In all such cases, however, the environmentally-produced dominance is more likely to crack under the strain than is a dominance based on a natural boldness and lack of fear.

2. *Assertion.* Several analytic studies have found a factor of 'dominance'. Cattell has repeatedly confirmed this factor and is able to provide some useful evidence as to the genetic component in this factor. His twin studies show that the genetic component is ten times as great as the environmental component in explaining differences between families. It would therefore appear that innate differences in anger susceptibility are the basis of one important dimension of

individual difference in the personality area. It is probable, however, that several drives may make some contribution to dominance (see below).

3. *Kindliness.* We have chosen this heading to refer to a factor which the Guilfords have called *agreeableness* and which Cattell names *cyclothymia*. Cattell has shown that it is largely dependent on hereditary influences, and we suspect that this hereditary basis is the parental drive. Teachers and housewives get the highest rating on this factor and this is certainly suggestive of some relation to the care of children. On the other hand it certainly influences much behaviour outside that immediately concerned with children. It contributes to interest in other people and probably is important in producing an attitude of sociability. It leads to consideration for the feelings of others and a general charitableness to human beings. It is negatively related to dominance and a study of leaders showed that their average scores were well below those of the general population.

DIFFERENCES AT TRAIT LEVEL

It should be remembered that, although we have been discussing differences with regard to drive strength, such differences are apparent only in the effects they have on learned traits, sentiments, or self-structure. Hereditary differences in the fear drive can be studied only by indirect means, and what will be obvious in the individual will be rather differences in a general trait of timidity resulting from the combined influences of his original fear drive and his experience. The particular forms which these traits take will vary from culture to culture according to the way of life, methods of child training, and the content of the moral code. We can mention here only major traits which develop in our own and similar types of culture. Some of these will appear in many cultures.

Sociability v. shyness*

We have already discussed this factor at the drive level. While largely influenced in its negative aspect by the fear drive, it is also considerably influenced by emotionality and tenderness. Highly emotional people are usually inclined to social activities but, if fear is strong, will be inhibited unless conditions are favourable. Environment may, therefore, be very important in establishing an early bias. Tenderness, too, will add to the desire for social contacts and, if conditions are favourable, may offset some natural timidity.

Dominance

This is related to sociability and the major influences are probably the degree of fear and anger drives operating. Where fear is low and anger high, the developing child is likely to find drive satisfaction through the control of others. This will be particularly so where tenderness is also lacking, so that there is less incentive to consider the feelings of others. Low emotionality may also contribute in this direction. Both of these influences will be important in developing a dominance as opposed to a sociability trait, though, of course, there is nothing to prevent a dominant person from also being highly sociable. The point is that a person who is too timid to develop a dominance trait may become highly sociable and a person who is bold enough to develop dominance may show little sociability.

These two traits of sociability and dominance bring out in an interesting way the difference in patterning at the two levels. It is the environmental situation which poses for the individual the choice of being sociable or not and the choice of being dominant or not. The adjustment that he makes to these two problems depends upon the relative strength of

* Cattell's *Parmia* v. *Threctia*.

his drives, the level of his aptitudes and his bodily capacities on the one hand, and the nature of his early experiences in terms of which he structures his reference frames, on the other hand. His early attitudes generalize into traits and these will have to be reckoned with in all further development. Once he has accepted a submissive position among highly dominating siblings or peers he will tend to continue this attitude later.

*Introversion–extraversion**

Jung has made this one of the most widely used dimensions for studying personality. One of the major attributes of the extravert is sociability while the introvert is shy. The central feature of the concept, however, is the tendency of the introvert to compensate for his lack of practical and social success by thinking. He tends to think about himself, to indulge in fantasy satisfaction of his drives or to substitute academic for practical success. The extravert makes love while the introvert writes love poems. The extravert also thinks but his thinking is always closely related to reality.

This concept must be used with care. In the first place it must be remembered that we can describe people as introverted or extraverted only as we can describe people as tall or short: most people will be somewhere between the two extremes. In the second place the concept is a complex one and, as usually used, involves a group of traits with varying emphasis upon the various constituents. It may be convenient to present the chief of these in a table:

Introvert

Shy
Indulges in fantasy satisfaction
Self-conscious
Favours contemplative occupations
Imaginative

* Cattell's *Autia* v. *Praxernia*.

Extravert

Sociable
Little fantasy
Absorbed in action
Favours practical occupations
Matter-of-fact

As soon as one sees these traits set out in this way one thinks of people who have some traits from one list and some from the other. It might, therefore, be more satisfactory to use the term *introversion* in a rather restricted way to refer only to what Guilford has called *thinking introversion*, which he has found to come out as a distinct factor in analysis. This, and the social factor, cover most aspects of introversion–extraversion as usually described and form a much safer descriptive system, since a person may be strongly biased to thinking rather than overt action and still show considerable sociability. Many poets have been of this type: highly sociable but manifesting little practical aptitude.

Anxiety level

The three specific factors which we have just discussed all relate in some way to fear and anxiety, and now we have a fourth which has been established by careful statistical analysis. Whereas the previous three relate to typical ways of meeting environmental situations this one is more in the nature of a chronic emotional state. When fear has been stimulated the person is for some time in a physiological fear-response state and peculiarly sensitive to further fear stimuli. Where fear stimuli are frequent and, more particularly, where a basic ego threat is felt, there may be a chronic fear state which is frequently described as 'free-floating anxiety'. That is, anxiety is experienced without relation to a specific stimulus and there is a constant tendency to seize on any likely stimulus as a focus for the anxiety. Such a person is constantly on the look-out for a suitable object on which to project his anxiety.

Nervous tension*

Closely related to the last trait is another which might be well described in popular terms as 'ragged nerves', and which is the result of considerable emotional strain. Such a person is tense and 'jumpy', ready to flare into a temper or break down and cry at the slightest provocation. For most people this is a passing state rather than a trait, but where there is continuing strain the condition may become chronic. It will be noted that people with high emotionality are much more likely to suffer in this way and it is doubtful whether, in describing normal people, we need to refer to this trait if we have some measure of their general emotionality. It may be highly important, however, in referring to people who are suffering from psychological disturbances.

Defensive suspiciousness†

In its extreme form this is one of the major psychoses: paranoia, but it is quite common among 'normal' people. It has two main aspects: an exaggerated opinion of the self and a suspiciousness of others. The discrepancy between the self-evaluation and the social esteem enjoyed is attributed to the evil intentions of others. It is obviously a defensive type of response and should be considered in connexion with the discussion in Chapter 17.

Other specific traits

Many further traits have been isolated by factor analysis and more still by clinical studies, but, as we are concerned only with major traits which are well attested, we shall ignore them here.

* Cattell's *Ergic Tension*. † Cattell's *Protension*.

DIFFERENCES AT THE LEVEL OF SELF-IDEAL

Obsessional tendency, or super-ego reaction

This is a trait more agreed to in form than in name. The Freudians have long talked of what they call the 'anal character' because they attribute its development to toilet-training experiences. Feeding and toilet-training are major aspects of early child life and it is understandable that attitudes developed then may become major traits for later life. Claims such as are made for this theory are exceedingly difficult to validate. We certainly find that doggedness, thrift, and orderliness tend to appear together, but there is some difference of opinion as to whether this is simply the result of toilet-training or whether it is not just a matter of these qualities first being manifested in connexion with the child's reactions to toilet-training. We can, perhaps, safely say that innate differences in children will make them react to toilet-training in different ways and that rigid toilet-training is likely to exaggerate the so-called qualities.

The obsessional tendency might be regarded as an attempt to achieve security. A person with this trait strongly developed places excessive emphasis upon the need for order in the world. Everything must be in its right place and so under control. Any sort of confusion is a security threat. The obstinacy which is also evident may be a similar expression of the need for order. The behaviour planned must be carried out because to change the plan is to introduce confusion and insecurity. Thrift also is related to this same security need since it signifies a greater control over the environment.

In Cattell's analysis the factor which seems to correspond to this is one which he has described as 'super-ego strength'. It appears to involve the setting of high moral standards with some evidence of perseverance and caution. We might postulate that the stress on moral standards is related to the initial formation of the super-ego, which we have already described as arising from the child's efforts to retain parental love and approval. A child experiencing high anxiety may react by setting himself a very high level of aspiration in the moral sphere so as to be sure of parental support. He thus develops a very strong need to be correct, and it is this which appears to characterize the obsessional person. Specific forms of obsession are probably related to propitiation needs with regard to experienced guilt. This may account for the fact that some people may show exceptional obsessional tendencies in one area (as punctuality) but none in another area (such as personal tidiness). Usually, however, there is a general tendency over a wide area.

It should be noted with regard to perseverance that this is not a long-term form relating to ego-achievement but perseverance on principle. It is interesting to note that a study of famous research workers showed them to be appreciably below average on this factor. This was probably because *their* perseverance was restricted to ego-involved situations. The person who perseveres on principle will often find he is wasting time on something which does not really matter to him. To be effective perseverance must be selective.

Ego-drive

This is not such a well attested factor as the emotionality factor, but it has similar generality and is now well recognized in research. Apart from the findings by formal factor analysis, it seems to have been recognized for a long time under guise of persistence.

In making a study of investigations into the nature of persistence the writer found that two major concepts appeared to be involved. The first related persistence to ego-involvement. People persisted at a task because they had made a self-investment in it. A mathematician would stick doggedly to a problem of a mathematical nature because he felt his reputation was at stake, but might quite easily give up a crossword puzzle. The second source of persistence seemed to have no relation to ego-involvement at all. Some people appeared to persist at a task which would bring them no self-enhancement just because they could not give it up. In fact they would continue with the task when it was obviously interfering with an important ego-involved task. Such people seemed to be just dogged. Their persistence required no effort, in fact they were powerless to oppose it or, at the best, could leave the task only by a great effort of will. This is the obsessional factor already described.

It is the first of these concepts which appears to be involved in the factor we are now considering. It depends for its importance upon the development of an organized self-system, but it is also possible that its strength is important in the actual formation of the self-system. It involves the achievement aspect of self which is so profoundly influenced by social approval. To what extent this achievement motive is present before parental approval begins its work is difficult to estimate and perhaps not very important. The outcome at least is a strong need for achievement which comes to be measured in terms of its effect on self-enhancement. The degree to which this need is present in people varies widely and is doubtless influenced by many factors. The degree of physical energy available may be important since, with abundant energy, the effort to achieve is much easier so that a higher level of aspiration may be set.

Ego control

This is the complement of emotionality with regard to control of behaviour. High emotionality results in unstable and inconsistent behaviour because the immediate drive strength is over-valued and so difficult to control. The same result will obtain if the control function itself is too weak. It is very important to notice that while low ego control and high emotionality have similar effects they are functionally very different. The ability to stop a car depends partly on the power of the engine and the speed which it may have produced and partly how efficient the brakes are. Poor brakes may suffice if the car never gets beyond a crawl; very efficient brakes may be necessary with a very powerful car which is likely to attain high speeds. For the psychologist it is therefore important to distinguish between the two aspects. If a patient's behaviour is well controlled one needs to know whether it is because he has high ego control or because there is little drive force for him to contend with.

Despite the enormous amount of clinical work done in this area we are still without any clearly understood concepts. Clinicians have been concerned with their particular patients rather than with general principles and there has been too little systematic research in the investigation of broad principles. All would be agreed that there is a control function along the lines we have described but some psychologists would argue that this is essentially a super-ego control or a broad self-sentiment control. Evidence from factor analysis, however, seems to indicate that there are several factors concerned as we have already indicated. There would seem to be some merit from the point of view of practical application, in trying to measure a positive control dimension which would correspond rather to the old concept of strength of will. There is some evidence that many people seek to control their behaviour as an end worth while in itself. The sort of control effect produced may finally depend upon the precise nature of the self-sentiment or the super-ego but the degree of control may be assessed without reference to the form of the controlled response. Whether this control function should be regarded as *part* of the self-sentiment or something independently formed will have to be decided in the light of later research and is not of pressing practical importance.

Self-sentiment

So far as measurement is concerned the self-sentiment may need to be sectioned into several parts. At least we shall need to take separately the material and moral aspects of self-aspiration and it may be necessary further to divide the moral aspect into ideal and super-ego components. No quantitative measure can encompass all that is involved in this reference frame. It is the qualitative detail which matters. However, we can gain a lot of useful information from knowing the relative importance of major areas. We could, arbitrarily, divide up the area into various logical sections but if we want our measures to have the maximum meaning we should make use again of the methods of factor analysis. If we find only one factor then one dimension will suffice. It would appear that several substantial factors are involved.

Material aspiration. There would appear to be good evidence for the existence of a sphere of material aspiration which tends to centre round the notion of career.

Moral aspiration. We have already suggested that the major difference between this and the area of material aspiration is that success is regarded as much more under the control of the individual. We cannot all produce world-shaking inventions or win international acclaim for singing or for writing poetry or for playing football but we can all observe a required moral code. We may be relatively stupid and that is unfortunate but we don't need to be dishonest.

Now it is interesting to notice that the moral code may present itself to us in various guises. We may think of doing our *duty*, not deviating from the straight and narrow path of righteousness, observing all the injunctions of 'Thou shalt not!'. This seems to be the essential aspect of the super-ego and may be what chiefly distinguishes it from the moral ideal which seeks the positive end of *goodness*, a process which may permit more gradations of success and so be more akin to the material type of aspiration. Both duty and goodness, however, have in common the notion of principles of behaviour. One may sometimes find opposed to these abstract requirements the demands of *personal loyalty*. Should you conform to the moral requirement of truthfulness or shield your friend? Personal loyalties for some people loom up very large and they would regard it as selfish to try to preserve their moral integrity at the price of the welfare of someone they loved. This too becomes a form of goodness, an ideal of behaviour.

It is possible that other personality traits may bias an individual towards abstract principles or personal loyalties as the basis of his ego ideal. Strong emotion and affection may encourage stress on loyalty; cold, unemotional types may favour abstract principles. There is some evidence in factorial studies for cold attachment to duty on the one hand and warm loyalty on the other.

Surgency. This is a factor in personality which was glimpsed quite early in research, the first indication being in the work of Webb which provided the first evidence of general emotionality, but it has never really jelled satisfactorily. It is characterized by optimism, freedom from care and worry, and by high verbal fluency. Burt found a factor of *euphoria* which highlights the first of these; Guilford found *rhathymia* which stresses the second (freedom from care); and Freudian theory has provided us with the notion of an 'oral' type which links optimism with verbal activity via the pleasant oral experiences of the child. In contrast to this 'nurture' explanation we have Sheldon's constitutional contribution.

Sheldon, by a process of analysis akin to the factorial approach, established the existence of three basic constitutional types: the *endomorphic* with a predominance of fatty tissue;

the *mezomorphic* with predominance of muscle; and the *ectomorphic* with long bones and little fat or muscle. Each of these he found to be associated with typical personality traits. Endomorphs were easy-going, optimistic, fond of company and eating, talkative and friendly. Ectomorphs, on the other hand, tend to be shy and restrained while mezomorphs are active, energetic, practical people. The correlation between Sheldon's physical types and personality types was doubtless much exaggerated by his failure to have the two sets of assessments done by independent workers but there is some evidence that the relationship does hold to some degree.

It would be tempting to conclude that there are three basic sources of differences in human beings and that these manifest themselves in both physical and mental aspects, but other evidence forbids such a view. It seems likely that the relationship between personality and physique probably derives from a variety of sources. People who don't worry may be fat because of that and they may be talkative and friendly because they can relax. It is worth noting, however, that endomorphy is definitely a feminine trait, the sex differences being quite pronounced, and that the warm friendliness of the endomorph could possibly be a manifestation of high parental drive.

Leaving aside for the moment the particular problem of constitutional linkage with some aspects of surgency we shall speculate that there are two explanations to be offered here and that there may well be two highly correlated surgency factors. One of these we shall take to be the result of ego-involved achievement. Pleasant hedonic tone is always associated with the successful outcome of activity but ego-involved behaviour has particularly far-reaching effects in this way and produces a very pervasive hedonic tone. When this is high there is a strong tendency to seek the company of others and to communicate; when it is low the tendency is reversed. We thus have a euphoric feedback effect which is relatively stable over time because of its relation to the ego system. Notice also that when we are thus elated by ego achievement we tend to see the world through rose-coloured glasses while the corresponding failure produces depression and pessimism. The person whose ego-involved hopes have been dashed sees not only the immediate failure but regards himself as a failure generally. His outlook is markedly pessimistic.

If this were the whole story with regard to surgency we should have to concede that genetic components are negligible or at least that people do not differ appreciably in the degree to which they react to success or failure. That they do differ seems fairly certain, so it would seem likely that we have to postulate a further surgency factor which is of the nature of what we have called a trait, a behavioural tendency resulting from the conditioning of a drive and the interaction of genetic and learning contributions. We are inclined nevertheless to consider the ego relationship to be fundamental and so we list surgency also among our ego components.

Our sketch of the ego components is now as complete as we are at present able to make it. Systematic, quantitative psychology has eschewed this region of voluntary decision and concentrated on simpler aspects of conditioning, so we have still a long way to go before we can develop adequate measures of individual differences in this area. The immediate future may bring some important contributions.

15

RACE AND SEX DIFFERENCES

Long before the question of individual differences was given any scientific treatment people were interested in race differences. It was commonly believed that there were wide differences between one race and another, both in ability and personality. The need for scientific study, however, was not felt. It was so obvious that all other races were so infinitely inferior to our own that scientific study was unnecessary. They were not even the same colour and they always spoke some barbaric lingo instead of our own language. Where they did attempt to speak our own language they were hopelessly inferior. This attitude has so much in common with the geocentric notion of the universe that it might be suspect for that reason alone. The idea that the universe revolves round our earth is not so very different from the idea that our race has a monopoly of all the virtues.

The idea of one's own racial or national superiority would be less disturbing if it were not held by so many different peoples. We can't all be so very superior. The myth of Nordic superiority, at least in its extreme form, has passed with the collapse of Nazism. Such an extreme view can now be easily held up to derision, but we still have many lesser forms of the same attitude. To what extent is there any justification for such views? Which, if any, is the superior race?

Psychology should have some answers here, but the matter is by no means simple and involves some really difficult problems which are not obvious to the layman. We must first decide what we mean by 'a race'. Then, since we cannot study every individual in the race, we must decide how we are to get a representative sample. Next comes the question of what we shall measure. Here we have made rather more progress, but the next problem of how we shall measure is much more difficult, as we shall soon see. Finally we have to consider the validity of our measuring instruments and so the confidence we can place in the results. We shall take up each of these questions in turn.

WHAT CONSTITUTES A RACE?

For the layman the answer to this is easy. There are five races: white, yellow, red, black, and brown. It is just a matter of colour. But there are some negroes who are lighter in colour than some of the so-called whites, and we are not referring to half-castes here. Europeans who live in hot countries acquire brown skins, and even sun-bathing enthusiasts in Europe acquire a tan. Do they thereby change their racial affiliation? Thus challenged, we are inclined to admit that we are concerned with more than the colour of the skin and begin to mention differences in hair and eye colour, shape of nose, length of limbs, etc. Let us consider some of these.

Three main forms of hair can be distinguished: straight, curly, and woolly. In colour it may be blond, brunette, or red. On this criterion the Australian blacks would be classified with Europeans rather than with negroes. Hair colour would subdivide Europeans but would lump all others together as brunettes. Eye colour, which is undoubtedly hereditary, would fail to give anything but the coarsest groupings.

Much use has been made of what is called the *cephalic index*, which is obtained by dividing the breadth of the head by its 'length' measured from forehead to back, and multiplying by a hundred, after the manner of the I.Q., to avoid fractions. On the basis of this measurement people are divided into dolicephalics (longheads) and brachycephalics (broadheads). This is one of the most reliable anthropometric measurements, but it does not effectively distinguish whites from yellows or blacks, so still leaves us with conflicting criteria.

More recently considerable attention has been paid to blood groups as a basis of classification. It is now well known that blood can be classified into several types and much attention has to be paid to this when transfusions are made. Certain mixtures are fatal and it is this which has developed interest in this area of investigation. Blood types conform to rigorous laws of heredity and might therefore be expected to be reliable indices to racial affiliation. Here again, however, we are faced with conflicting evidence. Japanese and Germans, Poles and Chinese appear with similar blood groupings. In no case is a blood group identical with a suggested race and the peoples of all countries belong to a variety of blood groups. As we discover more about blood groups and their distributions in various parts of the world, however, the possibilities begin to look more promising. Typical patterns appear to be emerging.

To the blood group evidence we may add other hereditary characteristics. An interesting one is the ability to taste PTC (phenyl-thio-urea) which is absent in American Indians and possibly in Mongolians. This ability is dependent on the presence of a particular gene at conception. It begins to look as though we can eventually work out a distribution of races in terms of the presence or absence of a number of easily identified genes which determine blood group or other obvious characteristics. Working on this basis Boyd has distinguished five major divisions of the existing races based on patterns of nine such criteria.

European with the highest incidence of Rh negative and high Rh_1 and A_2.

African or Negroid with extremely high Rho and moderate frequency of Rh neg. with rather high B.

Asiatic or Mongoloid with high A_1 and B and highest known incidence of the rare gene Rhz.

American Indian with no A_2 and probably no B or Rh neg.

Australoid group with high A_1, no A_2 or Rh neg. but high N.

The first three of these are generally accepted on various other grounds. The Australoid has tended to be grouped with one or two other groups and has usually been distinguished from the Negroid. The American Indian has frequently been grouped with the Mongoloid but is certainly distinguishable by physical characteristics.

It will be obvious to the reader that scientific racial classification is only in its early stages, that only the main subdivisions have been tentatively mapped out, and that we are hardly in a position yet to decide who is to be compared with whom in any investigation of superiority.

SAMPLING PROBLEMS

When we are dealing with large groups such as races it is obviously impossible to make a detailed study of all persons concerned. Resort is, therefore, had to sampling of some kind in much the same way as the grain buyer examines a small quantity of his commodity and so judges the whole. Such sampling can be very misleading, as one learns from an unscrupulous fruitseller who covers the top of a basket of strawberries with the more luscious berries and hides the poorer ones underneath. The grain buyer takes no chances like this, but takes his sample from internal portions of the sack, and probably also from several sacks chosen at random. If the sample is to be of any use one must be certain that it reflects the sort of variation which occurs within the total population. Sampling people in a city will certainly be misleading if we just take a hundred people within a given residential area. One area might be a slum and another restricted to highly successful business and professional people. On the other hand if we have a list of the inhabitants in alphabetical order and choose every hundredth name on the list we are likely to have a representative sample.

The sampling problem is so important with regard to this question because most of the comparisons of races have been carried out within a single country. There are special reasons for this tendency, as will be seen when we come to study the problems of measurement. For various reasons it is tempting to carry out research in a country like the U.S.A. where people of many races are to be found. There are many Negroes in the United States and they speak English, so it is tempting to compare their test results with those of white Americans and, so far as race sampling is concerned, this is probably quite legitimate since the way in which these Negroes were brought to America probably ensured that they were fairly representative of their race. There are other problems here, however, e.g. educational background and cultural differences (see later). So far as other national groups within the U.S. are concerned there are grave doubts as to the degree to which they represent their race or nation. Selective factors are always at work. We frequently find that the more successful people in a country tend to remain there whereas the less successful decide to try their luck elsewhere. Such people are not necessarily inferior but they are likely to have suffered from some handicaps, either in endowment or education, and, if they are taken as representative of their country, very distorted results may be obtained.

Other immigrants may come because they are more progressive and adventurous than usual and here the sampling may be biased in the reverse direction. Or they come because of some persecution at home. The factors involved are so many that all we can be sure of is that some sort of bias in sampling is certainly present but of the direction or amount we must remain in doubt. Under such conditions it is probably a waste of time to compare such immigrant groups and the evidence which has been obtained in this way is useless.

College students provide the most convenient source of subjects for psychological measurement, but quite obviously selective factors are at work in the choice of students in different countries and among different nationalities within the same country. Comparative figures based on students are, therefore, very suspect and quite inconclusive.

The selective factors operating in regard to students are absent in another group – army intake in time of war – and much has been made of results of testing U.S. recruits. Evidence from the First World War is here invalidated because of lack of uniformity in testing. That from the Second is sounder on the testing side but subject to all the objections we have mentioned with regard to immigrant groups.

Racial comparisons have sometimes been made in terms of the incidence of crime in two groups within the same country. It requires little knowledge to see the futility of this. For first-generation and second-generation immigrants it may be just the effect of being an immigrant with all the attendant problems of adjustment rather than belonging to a particular race. So many variables must be controlled before we can even say with confidence that racial origin has anything to do with it that the situation seems hopeless, and even if we could establish that racial origin was significant we would still be faced with the old bogy of selective immigration.

We are forced finally to the conclusion that the only effective sampling is random sampling within each race under its native conditions. Such sampling is easy but leaves us with other problems.

DIMENSIONS TO BE MEASURED

Obviously what we are interested in are the major dimensions which are genetically determined, but we are only just approaching any real agreement in this area. A reasonable scheme is now available with regard to aptitudes but there would be much disagreement with regard to personality. The result is that the only consistent work that has been done is with regard to sensory discrimination and intelligence. Many studies have been carried out in the personality field and these have established important differences with regard to affective reference frames, but it has been quite impossible to establish any genetic differences.

PROBLEMS OF MEASUREMENT

This area just bristles with difficulties. Since intelligence has been the chief dimension so far studied let us consider some of the difficulties in its measurement.

Motivation

We can expect valid comparisons from our intelligence tests only if both our groups are motivated to the same degree. Normally this is not a problem at all because most people are so concerned to show that they have high intelligence. The situation is different, however, when we come to extend our testing. Old people are likely to be less motivated than young people, and persons who have had no contact with academic work since they left school may label the testing as an academic activity and so one in which they cannot now be expected to do well. Having thus excused themselves, success is not important and they may make less than maximum effort. When we get away from our own country further complications may arise. Among some people it is considered very bad form to do better than your neighbour so that testees make sure there will be an adequate number of errors in their work to ensure they will not be outstanding!

Familiarity with form

There is no doubt that familiarity with tests generally produces an increase in the capacity to do tests. This is commonly referred to as 'test sophistication', and it certainly gives an appreciable advantage to persons who have frequently been tested. They have a better reference frame and are able to perceive faster what the tester is looking for. They are less likely to be upset by emotional factors.

Language difficulties

The handicap of having to use a language other than one's native language is obvious, but for the bilingual even testing in the primary language may be handicapped. The person who has to learn two languages is advancing on a dual front and, for a given vocabulary level, needs to be familiar with twice as many words. This makes greater demands on learning and, during some stages at least, must reduce efficiency. There are also conflicting principles involved in the two languages and this must sometimes result in a conflict situation. In New Zealand one notices that the younger or less-educated Maoris have their form of speech modified by the structure of their own language and this even when they speak English considerably better than they speak Maori.

Educational background

This is specially important in tests which depend upon knowledge of verbal material as do all the Binet revisions. With greater opportunities for education the vocabulary increases. Such education need not involve school attendance. Children of professional people have much more opportunity to extend their vocabulary than have children of labourers, even if they attend common schools. Klineberg found that the Southern-born Negroes show a surprising rise in I.Q. after some years of residence in New York (twenty-two points in eight years).

The problem of standardization

This is the outstanding difficulty in all inter-racial comparisons. We have already seen that it is necessary to test each racial group in the home country and in the native language. There is more involved in this than simply translating a common test into several languages. Even with a purely verbal test the word which has a similar meaning in another language does not necessarily have the same difficulty. Sometimes there is no equivalent word. The Eskimo has no general word for snow but has several words referring to specific forms of snow for which we have no terms. In translating, therefore, one has to choose a form in the new language which has the same difficulty as in the original. But the only way to decide that it has the same difficulty is to show that the same proportion of people can deal with it.

This situation applies to the test as a whole. Raw scores mean nothing. The reader will remember that mental ages were determined by choosing the questions which could be answered by the *average* child at each age. If we are translating these items into Uranian we can only be sure the translation is of equivalent difficulty if it also is answered by the average child of that age. But if it is, then British children and Uranian children will necessarily get similar results with the test on the average. By the very way in which we have constructed the test we have made sure that there can be no national or racial differences! We are thus in a really vicious circle. Either we use an untrustworthy test or we find no possible inter-racial differences.

Attempts have been made to produce 'culture-free' tests

which do not depend upon words and which can be expected to produce similar results despite language differences and differences in general background knowledge and customs. Some of these look quite hopeful but are not so successful in practice. The writer, who had a number of foreign students in a class, used one of the best known of such tests to minimize language difficulties and give the students an opportunity of making the best possible showing. The usual verbal test was also given when other students were taking it. It was rather disconcerting that the foreign students did better with the latter test, despite a poor knowledge of the language, than with the 'culture-free' test!

What we have to remember is that ability to solve problems depends upon the total cognitive reference frame and this may be very different with people growing up among different surroundings and customs. Habits of thought may be quite different, particularly as regards stresses on concrete or abstract constructs. There may be different attitudes about even attempting to solve problems. One people may learn always to attempt to solve its own problems while another may be accustomed to leaving such things to acknowledged experts. All these things contribute to the total effect and introduce differences which cannot be attributed to any genetic differences.

ACTUAL FINDINGS

We have spent most of this chapter stressing the difficulties in assessing race differences because this is the most important thing to be reported so far. For the most part we can only say that we don't know what race differences there may be. Certainly there is no strong evidence that any race is superior in any respect. In the sensory field where we can make use of reliable tests it is found that, despite the frequent assertion that primitive peoples have better discrimination, there is no indication of any significant differences. Such differences as are found are due not to sensory acuity but to more appropriate reference frames. The marvellous ability of the black tracker in Australia is paralleled by the doctor's capacity with a stethoscope. In both cases the development of the appropriate constructs makes possible unusual feats of perception.

On the question of intelligence the available evidence suggests that racial differences do not exist where fair tests are used. A comparison of Maoris with white New Zealanders using the Wechsler Bellevue test showed that with all the verbal tests the Maoris were definitely inferior, but with the more practical *performance* tests there was no significant difference between the two races. Similar findings have been made in comparing Indian with U.S. whites. Generally the indications are that 'g' is at very similar average levels in most races. Quite definitely we have no reason to assert the contrary.

With regard to other aptitudes and traits, we must still await evidence. In view of the different physical patterns found in different parts of the world it would seem unlikely that we should not find different aptitude patterns and even different temperament patterns. Although all human beings are essentially of the same species, there has evidently been sufficient operation of local selective factors to produce different tendencies in physiological development (e.g. compare the light-boned Hindu with the thick-limbed Maori) and all that we know of the effects of selection on psychological qualities suggests that some degree of differentiation has taken place here. Anyone who bases his attitude to racial equality on identical average values for all characteristics is making a poor bet which is only possible in our present state of ignorance. That all racial patterns of equipment will prove, on the average, of equal efficiency and value is very likely. That the patterns themselves will turn out to be identical is rather unlikely but, of course, by no means impossible. The situation with regard to sex differences may be a pointer with regard to the likely situation. Here we know a little more. We must now take up this topic.

SEX DIFFERENCES

There are many pitfalls in assessment here, but nothing like the difficulty we experience in race comparisons. We have to allow for different types of experience had by males and females, e.g. playing with dolls as opposed to mechanical toys. We have to allow for facts such as earlier school-leaving by the duller boys. But, with all due allowance made, there do appear to be quite significant differences. At the physiological level we have obvious differences with regard to stature and amount of subcutaneous fat. We find that girls develop faster than boys, attain physiological maturity earlier and live longer.

As in the case of race comparisons, we find no significant difference with regard to sensory acuity, with one exception. Females are less subject to colour-blindness and generally appear to have a better appreciation of colour qualities. This may be partly a result of greater interest in colour due to temperamental and environmental factors. Women's clothes are much more concerned with colour than are those of men and so there is more practical demand to study colour and build up a suitable reference frame.

When we come to consider the primary aptitudes there appears to be a clear-cut pattern. Women excel in perceptual speed and in verbal ability, particularly the latter. They learn to talk earlier and at all stages show superiority in the handling of words. Boys, on the other hand, show superiority in spatial ability and number ability, although at some ages girls may be in the lead with the latter. In school subjects the girls are superior in all language studies, while the boys beat them in maths and science. Girls also have an advantage in memory, but this may be due to their verbal superiority since the evidence is not so consistent with rote memory tests.

We have said that the pattern is obvious with regard to aptitudes, but it will be noticed that we have gone on to talk of *abilities*. It is only at the ability level that we are at all definite and it is still possible that the differences may be explained in terms of different sex interests resulting in the better development of particular reference systems. When we have data from societies where sex interests are different (e.g. the Tchambuli where women are responsible for earning the family living while the men engage in artistic and non-essential activities), we shall be in a better position to judge.

In the matter of intelligence neither sex can claim any decided superiority. Where verbal tests are used the females may gain some small advantage, but when allowance is made for verbal-ability and spatial-ability differences men and women seem to be on a par. The evidence generally points to different patterns of ability, perhaps of aptitude, but no real superiority in either sex.

TEMPERAMENT DIFFERENCES

We are on much shakier ground here because of the lack of well-agreed temperament dimensions. Different investigators have used different methods of assessment and, in most cases, it is impossible to separate differences due to genetic factors from those due to learning.

In a study by Hartshorne, May, and Maller it was found that girls were more cooperative than boys, were more self-controlled, and showed more persistence. Males greatly exceed females among delinquents from school onwards. Girls manifest nervous habits more frequently than boys. Males are reported to be more aggressive. All this is typical of the sort of evidence we have. So far as actual behaviour tendencies in our Western culture are concerned, it is all very important, but to what extent it is related to any genetic sex differences we just don't know and can only speculate.

At the speculative level we would be inclined to suggest that women are more emotional than men. Many psychologists would query this but much evidence would suggest it and it would accord with lay impressions. We would suggest also that women tend to be more timid and less physically aggressive than men. Again much opposing evidence may be quoted but none, either pro or con, is at all firmly based and it can at least be pointed out that in most species it is the male who is more aggressive and, furthermore, that this aggression is related to sex hormones since deprivation of these leads to loss of aggression, e.g. the well known contrast between the bull and the steer.

At this same level we would suggest that women show more tenderness or parental feeling. This, too, is little more than a hunch and will be hotly contested by many who would attribute the difference to social expectation and training. There is not enough evidence to justify a conclusion either way. The answer must come from further research. The suggestions advanced here are little use except as hypotheses to be tested. Probably some of the evidence will be available within a reasonable time. We cannot hope so much in the matter of race differences.

THE PATTERNING OF
PERSONALITY

16

EARLY EXPERIENCE

THE type of personality which a human being develops depends upon not only the basic drives and capacities and the environment in which they have to develop, but also the order in which the former mature. Environment can exist only in relation to the capacities of the organism so that the effective environment of the young child is very different from that of the adult. Nevertheless it is the early experience which lays the basis for future development and so it becomes very important to study these early years in order to get some insight into the basic patterning of personality. Our knowledge in this matter derives chiefly from two sources: the studies of the psycho-analytic schools inspired by Freud, and the work of anthropologists who have studied child-rearing practices to explain intercultural differences in personality. One of the latter, Kardiner, introduced the term *basic personality* to apply to the fundamental patterning laid down in this way and the term has been widely accepted.

During the first year the life of the child revolves around the need for food and his prime point of contact with the world is through his mouth. The Freudians have, therefore, referred to this as the *oral stage* and describe the personality traits resulting from this period as the *oral character*. The next period is chiefly concerned with toilet training and so is known as the *anal stage*, with its corresponding *anal character*. There follow two further stages of major importance in Freudian theory, the *phallic stage* (immature functioning of the sex drive in various forms) which continues until about the sixth year and which, after a latency period, is followed by the *genital stage* at puberty. We shall discuss both these latter under the heading *Sexual adjustment*. Through all these stages the child continues to have important security needs the frustration of which may have important consequences and these we shall consider as *Security adjustment*. In a later chapter we shall deal with *Ego adjustment* and *Social adjustment*.

ORAL ADJUSTMENT

The adjective here is aptly chosen. Not only does the mouth provide the infant with the means of satisfying its most pressing need, hunger, but it is the major reference point for every external contact. Anyone who has experienced the way in which the infant puts every possible thing into its mouth will recognize the justness of the description. In so far as the hunger drive has any preformed response patternings, these are related to the mouth. The baby will suck in a reflex way even when not hungry, and the hunger seems to emphasize this kind of activity. Sucking in itself appears to involve some degree of satisfaction even when no food is obtained or when the infant is no longer hungry. It has been suggested that there is a reservoir of sucking activity at any given time and this needs to be exhausted. If the baby obtains sufficient food without exhausting this reserve of sucking activity he will want to go on sucking after feeding. Similar activity is manifested by many animals which will continue to suck at any nipple substitute after feeding. Calves which have been bucket-fed, and so have obtained in a matter of seconds as much milk as they would require minutes to extract from the cow's udder, will suck one another's ears vigorously for considerable periods.

Sucking, then, provides both hunger satisfaction and a direct satisfaction of its own. In addition there are taste satisfactions which add to the effective satisfaction of this oral activity. Presumably most babies find their own mother's milk to have an attractive taste, and later the infant finds many other substances to provide satisfying tastes when inserted in the mouth. This tendency to suck and to have differential taste responses can easily be seen to be useful ramifications of the hunger drive and to have selective value in the evolutionary process. At earlier stages of racial history babies which did not manifest a sucking response would fail to mature and perpetuate their kind, while those with perverted tastes would fall victims to poisons of various kinds.

Finally, we have to note another source of affective satisfaction in connexion with the mouth. This is the erotic satisfaction which has been greatly stressed by the Freudian school. They find several erotic zones in the body, contact with which produces that particular kind of pleasure which we associate with sexual satisfaction. For Freud all the affective satisfactions we have referred to are simply manifestations of libido, or sex instinct, and so no question arises as to why sexual satisfaction should be allied to hunger satisfaction, but for other psychologists this may be an important question. We should be inclined to argue that the hunger system and the reproductive (i.e. sex) system are two quite distinct systems, but that, since they operate through common organs and motor systems, some overlap and complication is possible. The same organ serves for urination and intercourse and this is typical of our constitution. The two areas outside the genital area itself which are most sensitive to erotic stimulation are the lips and the breast, and it is just these which are involved in oral satisfaction. Yet it is the breast of the baby which is *not* stimulated by early oral activity. One would hardly imagine that experience with the mother's breast would make that of the girl erotically sensitive when she matures. It would seem much more likely that the breast should be sensitive because of its own direct relationship to the reproductive process. This is confirmed by observation of bottle-fed babies.

Now what of the lips? The answer here seems to be a complicated one. In the first place we have to note that erotic sensitivity is diffusely distributed throughout the skin. Contact of the lover with any part of the skin is stimulating and this is likely to be exaggerated in the more sensitive areas such as the mouth and hands. That both of these latter may function as genital substitutes is witnessed by various forms of sexual perversion. It seems likely, therefore, that some degree of erotic sensitivity lies initially in these areas and that, at the more immature stage of sexual development, this may be more important than later. We thus have a fusion of sexual and non-sexual satisfaction associated with oral activity, thus accentuating its importance.

Two major effects are mediated by the high affectivity of oral behaviour. Its temporary frustration will engender powerful anger and aggressive tendencies, and its long-continued frustration, as when the child is weaned, may lead to persistent striving to regain it. Smoking and similar activities have been associated with this latter. Sucking at a cigarette or pipe provides a perfectly respectable substitute for teat or comforter and, even without the help of nicotine, is soothing and satisfying. Of course, we should probably smoke without this satisfaction. For the young man or woman it is essential to smoke in order to acquire prestige, and they would do it even if it hurt! However, the immediate effects, at least, are not hurtful, and once the habit is established it is difficult to break.

Much has been made in inter-cultural studies of the time of weaning. Early weaning has been associated with strong oral drives in later life, but it is not quite so simple as this. What matters is not so much the time of weaning as how the weaning is experienced by the child. In this respect both extreme pleasure in the feeding situation and frequent frustration in feeding appear to accentuate the trauma of weaning. Very late weaning certainly reduces the strain of the crisis, but this is late weaning such as is unknown in our culture, weaning after several years.

We can distinguish two distinct types of effect in connexion with suckling the baby:

Effects due to the nature of the feeding experience. Frustration during feeding produces resentment and biting activity which lays down a pattern for future aggressiveness. Unhampered happy feeding leads to placidity and an optimistic view of life and a carefree personality.

Effects due to deprivation of oral satisfaction. This leads to a pining for further oral pleasure and puts a premium on all kinds of oral activity. Among these activities is included talking but the writer is inclined to doubt the importance of oral factors in this connexion although quite prepared to admit that they have some influence. It is only too easy to show that certain conditions may produce particular effects and then, because no other causal factors have been suggested, to conclude that all such effects are produced in this way. This is a grave weakness in some areas of Freudian theory because of its rather one-sided development, but there are encouraging signs now of widening views. The gap between psycho-analysis and the more academic forms of psychology is decreasing with advantage to all.

Child-rearing practices among the Mundugumor, a New Guinea tribe, have been instanced as an example of the effects of frustration during suckling. The mother is impatient and eager to finish the feeding process and terminates the meal as soon as the baby ceases to suck. This puts a premium on vigorous sucking, which may defeat its own end by producing choking which angers both baby and mother. The suckling situation is usually one of tension, which develops aggressive attitudes such as are typical in adult Mundugumor personality. It should be noted here, however, that it is not only in the feeding situation that the Mundugumor child is subjected to aggression-producing behaviour. This is typical of the whole relationship between the child and the adult. Furthermore, the child is constantly presented with examples of aggressive roles in adult behaviour and these he naturally adopts in his effort to achieve adult status. This situation is probably typical of personality development. Early bias is presented in the child-rearing methods, and this is accentuated by any predisposing tendencies (e.g. unusual anger drive) and by reinforcing experience in later life.

Before leaving this discussion of oral adjustment we should draw attention to the fact that frustration may produce not active aggression but rather sulky negativism. Where the fear drive is active, either because of innate strength or because of environmental encouragement, aggression may be denied overt expression, but this is much more likely at a later stage, after weaning normally takes place in Western culture.

ANAL ADJUSTMENT

After food problems it is excretion which looms large in the life of the young child. In most cultures adult control of excretion is demanded and the excreta are regarded with some degree of disgust. The attitude of children, however, is markedly different. Excretion provides an anticipation of erotic satisfaction and the act gains some erotic significance. Even playing with excreta may have some degree of such significance. Some parents take a tolerant view of this while others oppose it rigorously. All parents tend to welcome the time when the child will gain control of excretory functions and so reduce the demands on parental care. It has been suggested that where toilet training is vigorously enforced, typical personality traits develop, e.g. excessive emphasis on cleanliness.

The actual traits developed during the anal stage will depend not merely on the emphasis placed upon training, but the sanctions invoked in training and the ease with which the child can comply. This last is important in connexion with the question as to when toilet training should commence. If training is emphasized before the child is ready he will be unable to comply with demands. Similarly, at a later stage constipation may prevent the child complying. In both cases there are likely to be emotional complications. The ideal situation appears to be one in which suitable toilet habits are encouraged but without any suggestion of punishment or active disapproval for failure. Under such conditions it is likely that very early training may not be harmful, may in fact condition suitable habits before conscious consideration can provoke undue emotional considerations. Where the child is able to achieve easy control of his excretory functions he will accept this as just another form of achievement and will tend to be optimistic and confident. At the same time he may come to regard his compliance as in the nature of a gift to the parent and the latter's approval may operate as a conditioning of generosity. The trend is thus towards a cheerful, generous, optimistic disposition with no encouragement of worry.

Punishment for non-compliance with toilet requirements is likely to invoke resentment if it is by way of chastisement and anxiety if by threatened loss of love. This will be exaggerated where the child has difficulty in complying either because of too early training or because of constipation. In this case physical punishment is likely to provoke an aggressive obstinacy and threat of love-withdrawal a sulky obstinacy. Sulkiness may be regarded as anger turned against the self as a means of expiating guilt and appealing to the love of the parent. It is not likely to arise where the child has not experienced parental love.

Even where the parents are careful not to threaten, the constipated child, who is unable to respond as required, may experience the situation as a threat if the parents manifest anxiety about the situation themselves. This is probably complicated by the probability that constipation may frequently itself be due to emotional disturbance. The constipated child is often already an anxious child, and this anxiety is accentuated by the toilet situation. Three major results may ensue. In the first place the child may develop an anxious persistence which merges into obstinacy where the situation is experienced as unduly threatening. In the second place a hoarding tendency may develop. This is related to the interpretation of faeces as a gift to the parents which we have already remarked on. The gift now, however, is regarded as a means of buying security and is equivalent to money put into the bank for similar purposes. There is thus a bias to save rather than to consume, and this can apply later to a very wide area, even to time which must never be wasted.

The third result is a reaction formation, i.e. a swinging in the opposite direction. The natural interest in excreta is replaced by a fastidious avoidance of all kinds of messiness. This is an excessive desire to please the parent. But this reaction is not restricted to the particular situation we have referred to here. It appears to come sooner or later in all societies where there is adult disgust towards excreta and parental permissiveness in this respect may only lead to a greater degree of reaction later when the child discovers what the parental attitude really is. In view of this it is by no means clear at the moment as to what aspects in toilet training account for the pronounced differences in adults with regard to orderliness and cleanliness. Probably more attention needs to be paid to other factors as we have suggested in our discussion of obsessional tendency.

SEX ADJUSTMENT

This heading could easily be misleading. We are not here concerned with the sexual satisfaction of the adult, but rather with the way the development of the child is complicated by sex drive in various forms and the way in which he is able to deal with the resulting problems. For the Freudian the two preceding sections of this chapter have already been concerned with this, but we prefer to consider the erotic element as only one factor in connexion with oral and anal adjustment. To some extent this is also true of the stage we are now to consider, but the sex drive may be regarded as playing a major role and will so justify our heading.

The first purely erotic stimulation may be regarded as that resulting from the child handling his (or her) own sexual organs. That this is in some degree pleasurable from the earliest years seems to be indicated by the degree to which it is indulged in. Parents, at least in our own culture, are embarrassed by this and seek to combat the tendency. Often they have threatened to 'cut off' the offending organ in the case of a boy. That this is no vain threat is confirmed for the boy when he sees his sister's or other girls' genitalia. In fact, even when no threats have been made, this latter event may well lead to the boy fearing castration while the girl may conclude that she has already been castrated. Thus Freud is led to postulate a *castration fear* in boys and a *penis envy* in girls.

The situation is complicated by the role of the mother and father. Each tends to be more attracted by the opposite-sex child in terms of the bias of their own sex drive, and so these opposite-sex relationships tend to be more tender. At the same time the developing child, searching for the prestige of adult status, tends to take the same-sex parent as providing a role model. The boy thus needs to replace his father in order to succeed and the girl to replace her mother, and a conflict situation is set up which is referred to as the *Oedipus complex* in the case of the boy and the *Electra complex* in the case of the girl (both names from Greek mythology). As described by Freud, the child has erotic desires towards the parent, and this has been violently objected to by many critics, to whom Freud has replied that the very violence of their protest is evidence of the truth of his contention that this state of affairs did exist in youth but was 'repressed' (forced out of consciousness) by the developing *super-ego* (moral reference frame). This, however, is the sort of argument that wins both ways and must be regarded as rather unfair. A careful examination of the facts seems to suggest that Freud is right in asserting that some sexual component enters into this situation, but that the major effects can be accounted for in terms and non-sexual factors. Jealousy of the father could be present in intense form without any sexual drive operating at all. If, in addition, we think of the sex component as largely tenderness with an opposite-sex bias (largely initiated by the parent) the hypothesis should be quite acceptable to anyone who has not himself had an unduly exaggerated Oedipal conflict!

This Oedipal (the term is often used to include the feminine counterpart) conflict becomes resolved by the child *identifying* with the same sex parent, substituting *we* for *I*. He takes over the parental moral code (technically known as *introjection*) which now governs his conduct as the super-ego. The child now seeks to behave in ways acceptable to the parents and, in particular, represses his pretensions towards the opposite-sex parent. So far as the sexual component is concerned, the process is hastened by the active discouragement by the parent of any sexually tinged behaviour. Freud finds the resolution of this Oedipal situation to be the focal point in the development of the moral self-reference frame and, provided one thinks of it *only* as a focal point, this is probably quite a reasonable assumption.

SECURITY ADJUSTMENT

Throughout this book we have stressed the fundamental importance of the striving for security. The happiness and efficiency of later life depends very much upon the early establishment of a feeling of security. Parents often sense this and strive to make their children independent and confident. The aim, however, is one that can easily defeat its own ends. The child who is given insufficient support becomes anxious and fearful, develops a basic insecurity which may dog him all his life. It is the experience of successful coping which builds up the feeling of security. A child should have every opportunity to do things for himself, but at the same time should be protected from frightening failure. Undue protection, on the other hand, has a similar effect in promoting insecurity. The child comes to depend on his parents rather than upon himself and whenever parental support is lacking he is thrown into a state of anxiety. Successful development depends upon a nice balance between the two extremes.

During the first year security depends wholly upon parental care and we have seen that this must involve more than simply meeting the physical needs of the baby. There must be loving care. And as the child grows older his demand for loving and not merely care becomes greater. The mother whose care is largely motivated by her own feelings of guilt because she did not want the child and resented its arrival may, despite her excessive solicitude for the child, fail to meet his love needs satisfactorily.

Although treatment of the child during the first year provides the initial bias towards security the need is a continuing one and the child may thus experience love deprivation at varying periods in its development. It is impossible to obviate such a feeling of deprivation by extra care and love during the early years since this only strengthens the love tie and makes the deprivation the more felt. Adler asserted that two types of children experienced love deprivation: those who were neglected and those who were spoilt. The latter came to expect so much that inevitably there came a time when parents or parent substitutes fell below this standard and the child reacted to this *relative* rejection. The advent of a brother or sister is, of course, critical in this respect, and a spoilt child can hardly avoid feeling rejected under these circumstances.

The stage at which deprivation is experienced is important with regard to the way in which the child develops. As we have seen, it may produce a fatal depression during the first year. Later the physical effects are not so pronounced, but the psychological effects are profound. One possibility is an increased emphasis on sensual satisfaction. This leads to unusual interest in the sex organs and the child, finding them so satisfactory himself, may display them to others. This may accentuate the sex drive later or may result in a generalized tendency to self-display without any direct sex reference.

A common response is that of aggressiveness. Denied love, there is a reaction of hate. Later, when the super-ego develops, this aggressiveness is repressed, but may then provide the motivation for various obsessional acts which are offered as a sort of propitiation. At the folk-lore level we have the saying, 'Step on a crack and break your mother's back', which epitomizes this sort of approach with its guilt propitiation, as do the many stories of wicked stepmothers, the hatred and feeling of rejection by the mother. It is because we all experience some degree of rejection at times that we are all able to appreciate the story of the wicked step-parent who, incidentally, almost invariably appears to be the mother.

Frequently sickness may be exploited to regain parental attention. This is likely when the child has experienced some sickness and discovered the increased attention which it brings. Under such circumstances there is a strong incentive to prolong the sickness and seize upon any new excuses for pleading sickness. This may lay down very important precedents for later life.

Rejection after the fourth year is likely to provoke an extremely independent attitude. 'I don't care' is the typical response. He cannot have love so denies his need for love. It easily leads to delinquency, particularly when there is a poorly organized ego system. When the ego system has already developed the child may respond by exaggerated efforts to earn approval as a substitute for love. He becomes the good child. Often this works well until later life. Hadfield tells of a girl who was an only child until the fourth year, but who was then very jealous of the baby rival. On one occasion, as she stood on the table, she threw her arms around her mother, who impatiently pushed her away. She fell but was little hurt except for her feelings. She decided to be independent. She helped the family and did very well at school and college. She then became a leading person in maternity and child welfare problems. The pattern of being good paid off well. Then she married a man with rather less personality than herself and set out to be the perfect wife and mother. The perfect parent stuff was wasted on her two children, however, who gave her no credit for her efforts, and at this stage she broke down with a bad neurosis.

17

EGO ADJUSTMENT

At each stage in his life a person has typical adjustments to make but always he is faced with the problem of ego adjustment. Once his self-reference frame has developed he is constantly faced with the problem of achieving an actual self commensurate with his level of aspiration or ideal self. When he finds himself slipping in this respect he experiences profound dissatisfaction and will resort to several methods of lowering his level of self-aspiration with the least damage to his self-esteem, or will endeavour to find some substitute satisfaction. A study of these throws important light on ego functioning. They are often referred to as *psychological mechanisms*.

SOUR GRAPES MECHANISM

This is well illustrated in the fable where the fox revises his conception of the grapes which he cannot attain. By regarding them as sour he is able to resolve his frustration. This is an exceedingly common process and is effective chiefly in lowering ego aspiration without loss of self-esteem. To relinquish an aim in which we have become ego-involved may be very painful, but, if we can convince ourselves that the original ego-involvement was a mistake due to our ignorance of the real nature of the goal, there is a minimum amount of disturbance. This is the 'sour grapes' approach. It is usually regarded cynically as a weak means of retreat, but it is often a quite realistic manoeuvre. The grapes may not always be sour but their sweetness is often very much over-rated by us when we first pursue them, and it is not only the fox which attains them! Contrariwise, the unsuccessful person may develop an exaggerated idea of the value of the unattained object. It makes for mental health if we can find the flaws in the unattainable.

Complementary to the sour grapes mechanism is one which has, by analogy, been christened the *sweet lemon* approach, where we concentrate on discovering the merits of what we can attain. Pollyanna in the book by Montgomery is an excellent example of this attitude towards life. No matter what happens Pollyanna is always able to be glad about something. Such behaviour may not always seem very realistic to us, but some of us could wish that more of our friends manifested it and that we ourselves were a little more capable of it. Of course, the danger here is that of unduly lowering our standards of aspiration. In our highly competitive Western world this may make us incapable of adequate effort so that we let down our families.

The setting of appropriate levels of material self-aspiration can be quite an important problem. Often people are very unrealistic about this. They may set themselves quite unsuitable tasks. A man with average, or less than average, intelligence may set his heart on being a doctor, or a girl with little more than average looks and no acting ability may aspire to Hollywood stardom. The results can easily be disastrous. The ability to assess our own assets and strive for reasonably ambitious goals with appropriate persistence is not easy. Many people dread an intelligence test, convinced that they cannot make an outstanding score but fearful of making a mediocre one. A realization that, after all, this is only one measure of ability and that they cannot adequately plan their lives without a realistic appreciation of all their abilities should do much to modify this attitude. Many world figures might cut little ice if evaluated merely by an intelligence test, but surely this does not in any way lessen their real worth.

RATIONALIZATION

Someone has said that there are two reasons for every action: the one given and the real one. Certainly we frequently delude ourselves with regard to our motives. The man who justified the low wage paid to his gardener on the grounds that poverty produces sturdy characters, and that more money would only be spent on luxuries, was certainly rationalizing, since he was not prepared to apply the same reasoning to himself. His own income was a high one and he spent much on luxury, but this was 'good for trade'! When we would like to go out to see a film we tell ourselves that rest and recreation are good for us. This happens to be true within certain limits, but this is typical of most rationalization. It has a rational basis. It is merely an attempt to find sound reasons for doing something which we wish to do anyway. Our behaviour is always dictated by affective factors, and our reasoning ability is employed to discover an appropriate means to the required affective satisfaction. But the barriers opposing such satisfaction may be internal ones. The contemplated action may conflict with our self-reference frame and is, therefore, unacceptable to us unless we can get round this conflict. Rationalization is one way of doing this, and in its general intention it is perfectly legitimate. The objection to it is that as soon as we find a reason that 'seems to hold water' we close down on the thinking process. We are too biased in our consideration of the evidence, and tend to make judgement in our own favour as soon as we find favourable evidence.

COMPENSATION

The mechanisms we have considered so far have been concerned with modifying the perception of an action or a goal so that it will be more acceptable to the ego. What we can't get is depreciated relative to what we can achieve, or, what at first sight seems incompatible with our self-ideal, is placed in another light where it appears acceptable. The mechanism we have now to consider tackles the problem from another angle. We sacrifice the unattainable or unacceptable goal, but console ourselves by achieving greater satisfaction in other, and, if possible, related, areas. Adler, who has paid much attention to this mechanism as a major factor in moulding what he called the 'life style', points to numerous cases of compensation carried to excess: over-compensation. He refers to the many men of small stature, such as Napoleon, who have become great leaders, to Demosthenes who overcame a speech defect and went on to become one of the world's greatest orators, to many famous artists who have suffered from defective vision. It is easy to find examples of this kind. Sandow, who overcame his physical weaknesses and achieved world fame as a 'strong man'; Gene Neely, who was stimulated by the loss of an arm to become a champion in several fields of sport; Helen Keller, who triumphed over crippling sensory defects. The list of even well known names is a long one. Examples among the less famous are inexhaustible. We have the coward who becomes a bully, the timid person who blusters, the person who feels inferior but adopts a highly dignified bearing, the mediocre person who is always boasting, and so on.

Compensation need not be in the area of inferiority, but it is preferred there since it more directly counteracts the feeling of inferiority. Gene Neely might have written books instead of playing football and billiards, but the latter was a more effective denial of his inferiority. In the same way Bruno Wintersteller, the Austrian skiing champion and alpinist, has been impelled to prove that, with the aid of special crampons, he can still conquer the Matterhorn. Walter Scott compensated in literary work for the disabilities he faced in the physical area, and this is probably a common factor in producing an introvert bias.

Compensation is not always of a positive kind. A frequent development is the substitution of *fantasy satisfaction*. The weakling cannot become a world-famous strong man but he can dream of this. The man who fails to attract feminine admiration may luxuriate in imaginary romance. The suburbanite who is denied adventure may seek it in imagination, and if his own imagination is insufficient he seeks the help of films and novels. We all tend to do this to some extent. We *identify* with the hero or heroine. For the time being we *are* the hero or heroine and get vicariously the satisfactions denied us directly. Since we are all denied some satisfactions to some degree this has attraction for us all. Such conduct is often derisively termed 'escapism' but a certain amount of this may be quite healthy. It ceases to be healthy when it interferes with the efficient facing of reality. If it soothes jaded nerves and enables us to return more effectively to the problems of practical living it is a useful tonic and none the worse for being enjoyable.

The form of modern city life necessarily induces strains which were not present in simpler times. The pace is faster but the range is often highly restricted and many of the primitive satisfactions may have to be sought in other forms. Escapism may thus become an essential part of healthy living, but when it becomes a substitute for practical action there is danger. In the extreme form we have people living in a completely unreal world, so cut off from reality that their physical needs have to be provided for by others. This divorce from reality is typical of the mental patient who is described as suffering from schizophrenia, popularly referred to as 'split mind'. This must be carefully distinguished from dual personality of the Jekyll-and-Hyde type. The split in schizophrenia is between thinking and practical action and not between two personality syndromes. It is quite possible that its more extreme forms are dependent on some organic disturbance. Certainly it should not be thought that anyone who tends to day-dream a lot is heading towards psychosis. Day-dreaming is only one of the symptoms; its causes lie much deeper.

We have referred above to identification as part of the compensation processes involved in fantasy. This mechanism may operate in other ways too. The football player tends to identify with his team, to speak of 'we' instead of 'I' and to gain from the victory of his team the same satisfaction that he would experience from a personal victory. In fact it *is* his victory because he has contributed towards it. But he may still think of it as his victory when he has not actually played in the team. When the school team wins, every member of the school has the experience of winning. When the national champion scores an international victory, it is *our* victory. It is through this process of identification that we get much of our satisfaction. Again the process can be quite healthy. The individual who is not able to make many identifications may be regarded as socially deficient and psychologically unhealthy. On the other hand, extreme identification fuses with extreme fantasy, as in the mental patient who tells us that he *is* Napoleon or Hitler.

REPRESSION

One way to dispose of conflict because of an unacceptable goal is to refuse to acknowledge its existence. The unmarried woman who feels that any thought of sexual satisfaction outside marriage is immoral may completely repress her sexual urges. In this way she is consciously rid of them, although they may still exert effects at the unconscious level – they may, for example, lead her to be highly critical of sexual lapses in others.

This process of repression must be carefully distinguished from inhibition or suppression. A person may experience a strong sexual urge and yet control it or he may experience strong resentment against his parents and yet deny it expression. In neither case have we repression. It is only when the mere entertainment of such feelings is felt as being too shameful to be tolerated with self-respect that repression ensues and the memory is pushed into oblivion. This is the fate of the Oedipal attachment according to the Freudian description. In the interests of the developing self the former goals are renounced and repressed, pride of place now being given to the parental moral code which becomes 'introjected' as the super-ego and so becomes the chief cause of future repression. This strengthening of the self-reference frame which takes place with the renouncing of a powerful conflicting motive is interesting. A similar result often ensues when the alcoholic conquers his craving and becomes highly religious.

DISPLACEMENT

A frustrated drive, instead of being repressed, may become displaced; that is, it may find expression in some other permitted direction so that it is no longer in conflict with the self-reference frame. The man who has to suppress his anger against his boss because of the dangerous consequences of its open expression may find an outlet in venting it on the office boy or on his wife. The occasion may be a minor episode which would normally provoke only slight resentment, but, once a legitimate excuse has been found, the flood of anger bursts forth to the astonishment of the unfortunate victim. This mechanism is an extremely common one, but might be regarded as of only passing importance and not related to important personality traits. It assumes importance in relation to another process. It has been suggested that the child is constantly being subjected to anger stimuli without being able to vent such anger. Parents are not only the chief sources of satisfaction for children but they are also associated with many frustrations. It is parents who are so frequently saying 'No!' to the child. When the anger consequent upon such resentment is repressed, it may still continue to act via the unconscious (i.e. at the affective level but without cognitive insight) and, in particular, it may be displaced. The hate which we direct towards the enemy during wartime may be regarded as a displacement of this kind. It may be quite out of relation to what is justified by the actual conduct of the enemy, but the situation is one which frees us from the need for repression, and all the hatred earned by our parents now finds legitimate outlet.

The peculiar situation that we consciously love and unconsciously hate our parents is often referred to as *ambivalence*. The two opposed forms of feeling are both potentially there and will manifest themselves according to the circumstances. This is one of the explanations why romantic love can so easily turn to hate. The hate was there from the beginning but was repressed. A turn of circumstances releases this repression and immediately we have a full-blown sentiment of hate.

PROJECTION

Closely related to displacement is the mechanism of projection. A person may have an undesirable trait such as meanness, which he is loath to recognize in himself because it would arouse feelings of guilt and the need for punishment. Self-punishment is seldom very satisfactory, whereas we frequently get pleasure out of punishing others. Under these circumstances the mean person may be unduly sensitive to this fault in others, whom he may criticize with undue satisfaction because he is really punishing himself but without the usual subjective inconvenience! This process of finding our own faults in others is referred to as *projection* and it may be indulged in with the flimsiest of reasons. A woman who was shown a series of ink-blots such as are used in the well-known Rorschach personality test exclaimed 'How dare you, sir! How dare you show such horribly indecent things to me?' She had read into them what was in her own mind and had attributed to the psychologist motives which she herself was repressing. So common is this attitude of projection that it has been said one should always suspect the person who frequently accuses others of some vice of having that vice himself. The person who never trusts others is probably not trustworthy himself. The person who is always accusing others of stealing must have some strong personal incentive to stealing. Those who constantly accuse others of immorality are probably of questionable morals themselves.

Projection is another mechanism which shows up strongly in wartime, since it too is provided with a convenient scapegoat. The enemy may be accused of all our own sins and we can expiate our guilt by punishing the enemy. The problem of ambivalence is conveniently solved. Our enemies are completely bad and our friends entirely virtuous. Whether, when the war is over, we are any the better for this emotional release or whether we have not incidentally built up new and even more dangerous anti-social traits is another question which we cannot go into here.

Some comment on the so-called 'projective tests' may be in order here. An example is the Rorschach ink-blot test to which we have just referred. The blots do not actually represent anything in particular, but, because of their vagueness, can be seen in various ways by different people, and the way in which they do see them is an indication of their personality. Only in a few cases, however, do we have projection of the sort we have referred to where someone else is accused of a fault which is actually present in the person herself. Most of the information of the Rorschach test comes from the particular way in which the person is led to perceive in terms of personality and mood. It is not projection in the clinical sense but only biased perception. We have tried to make clear earlier that all perception is biased. The projective tests merely reduce the objective reference to a minimum as in the ink-blot, in order to give the subjective elements full rein. It is a pity that the term projective became applied to them, but perhaps we can still preserve a clear distinction between this and the word *projection*, which should be reserved for the special significance which we have described.

SUSPICIONS AND DELUSIONS

When an individual fails to achieve hoped-for success there is a strong incentive to rationalize this as due to the deliberate efforts of others. It is said that a bad workman blames his tools. This is a convenient explanation of failure. Just so, the man who has failed to get a coveted job may assert that the successful person had a 'pull', or that someone has belittled his abilities. Some degree of this sort of thing is quite common, but this too is a mechanism which is exhibited in extreme form in our mental institutions. Schizophrenic patients may become quite convinced that some mysterious 'they' are constantly plotting against them, using radio waves to influence their thoughts, and pursuing their evil intent in the most fantastic manner. Such delusions are frequently linked with an exaggerated idea of the patient's own importance. This is easy because one thing explains the other: the patient may really be an important millionaire (on his own showing), but owing to the machinations of his enemies he is reduced to his present plight. This combination of inflated self-opinion and suspiciousness of the motives of others is typical of paranoia, and people showing a tendency in this direction are sometimes described as being paranoid. It will be remembered that we found this to be an important dimension in normal personality. It is possible that some people are constitutionally more prone to solve ego-conflicts in this way, but early patterning must be important too.

REGRESSION

Failure to secure ego satisfaction will sometimes result in reversion to an earlier stage of development. Sometimes this is actively encouraged by the environmental situation. The young child who finds the latest baby usurping all mother's attention may feel that he is no longer important. He contrasts the failure of his own more developed response patterns with the baby's appeal, and it seems quite reasonable that he should conclude he has overshot the goal! Not only is the later-developed pattern likely to disintegrate under the stress, but there is before him the direct model of successful behaviour at a more infantile level.

The tendency to regress under strain is always present. Hardened adults may at times break down and cry or, with frustration, give vent to temper tantrums. Sometimes the regression may be completely pathological. Nicoll reports the case of a war prisoner who reacted to guilt strain by regressing to the psychological age of five. He lisped and behaved in very similar manner to the actual behaviour at this stage of development. After two weeks at this extreme level he 'grew up' again to the age of seventeen. Regression of this type is important in so far as it tends to be permanent and in so far as it establishes patterns of behaviour for future occasions. If such lapses 'pay off' there will be greater tendency to employ them on future occasions of stress.

These are some of the major ways in which the ego manages to keep on terms with the self. It is impossible to make an exhaustive list, since they are limited only by the extent of human ingenuity. The ones listed, however, are so common that anyone who professes to have some insight into human nature must have some familiarity with them.

SUGGESTED READING

Anastasi, Anne, *Differential Psychology*, Macmillan Company, New York, 1958

Ausubel, D. P., *Theory and Problems of Child Development*, Grune & Stratton, New York, 1958

Bachrach, A. J., *Psychological Research*, Random House, New York, 1962 (paperback edition)

Bowlby, John, and Fry, Margery, *Child Care and the Growth of Love*, Penguin Books, 1953

Broadhurst, P. L., *The Science of Animal Behaviour*, Penguin Books, 1963

Brown, J. A. C., *The Social Psychology of Industry*, Penguin Books, 1954
Freud and the Post-Freudians, Penguin Books, 1961.
Techniques of Persuasion, Penguin Books, 1963

Cantril, Hadley, *The Why of Man's Experience*, Macmillan Company, New York, 1950

Cattell, Raymond B., *An Introduction to Personality Study*, Hutchinson's University Library, London, 1950
Personality and Motivation Structure and Measurement, World Book Co., New York, 1957
The Scientific Analysis of Personality (forthcoming in Penguin Books)

Drever, J., *A Dictionary of Psychology*, Penguin Books, 1952

Eysenck, H. J., *Uses and Abuses of Psychology*, Penguin Books, 1953
Sense and Nonsense in Psychology, Penguin Books, 1957
Know your Own I.Q., Penguin Books, 1962
Check your Own I.Q. (forthcoming in Penguin Books)

SUGGESTED READING

Flugel, J. C., *Man, Morals and Society*, Penguin Books, 1963

Fordham, F., *An Introduction to Jung's Psychology*, Penguin Books, 1961

Freud, Sigmund, *Psychopathology of Everyday Life*, Ernest Benn, 1960 (paperback edition)

Hadfield, J. A., *Dreams and Nightmares*, Penguin Books, 1954
Childhood and Adolescence, Penguin Books, 1962

Hall, Calvin S., *A Primer of Freudian Psychology*, New American Library, New York, 1955 (paperback edition)

Hebb, D. O., *Organization of Behavior*, Science Editions Inc., New York, 1961 (paperback edition)

Hilgard, Ernest R., *Introduction to Psychology*, Harcourt, Brace & Company, New York, 1953

Hunter, I. M. L., *Memory: Facts and Fallacies*, Penguin Books, second edition, 1963

Krech, David, and Crutchfield, Richard S., *Elements of Psychology*, Alfred A. Knopf, New York, 1958.

Lazarus, R. S., *Personality and Adjustment*, Prentice-Hall, 1963 (paperback edition)

Lorenz, Konrad Z., *King Solomon's Ring*, Pan Books, 1957

McKeller, Peter, *A Textbook of Human Psychology*, Cohen & West, London, 1952

Mace, C. A., *The Psychology of Study*, Penguin Books, 1962

Morgan, Clifford T., and Stellar, Eliot, *Physiological Psychology*, McGraw-Hill, New York, 1950

Sherif Muzafer, and Cantril, Hadley, *The Psychology of Ego-Involvements*, John Wiley & Sons, New York, 1947

Sluckin, W., *Minds and Machines*, Penguin Books, 1954

Stagner, Ross, and Karwoski, T. F., *Psychology*, McGraw-Hill, New York, 1952

SUGGESTED READING

Storr, Anthony, *The Integrity of the Personality*, Penguin Books, 1963

Thomson, Robert, *The Psychology of Thinking*, Penguin Books, 1959

Tyler, L. E., *Tests and Measurements*, Prentice-Hall, 1963 (paperback edition)

Valentine, C. W., *The Normal Child*, Penguin Books, 1956

Vernon, M. D., *The Psychology of Perception*, Penguin Books, 1962

Way, L., *Alfred Adler: An Introduction to His Psychology*, Penguin Books, 1956

GLOSSARIAL INDEX

ability, 193
aerial perspective, 157
affective differences, 197
affective reference frame, 100
anal adjustment, 240–3
anal character, 235
anal stage, 235
anxiety, 119, 208
aptitude, 193
assertion, 204
autonomic system, 66: a major division of the nervous system. It controls functions such as perspiration, blood supply to the surface of the body, salivation, heart rate, etc. Psychologically it is important for its mediation of the physiological responses in emotional states

basic personality, 235

canalization, 104: the establishment of a preference for certain modes of drive satisfaction, e.g., the development of food habits
cathecting, 105: the attachment of affect to a perceptual or motor response
common movement, 158
compensation, 250
conditioned drive, 83
conditioned response, 86

conditioning, operant, 84: the process of (a) attaching a new stimulus cue to a reflex or drive, or (b) of attaching a new motor response to a drive
classical   = (a) above
instrumental ⎫
operant   ⎬ = (b) above
respondent ⎭
conscience, 127
constancy (size and brightness), 159: the perceptual phenomenon whereby objects tend to appear their usual size or brightness irrespective of size of retinal image or changes in illumination

day dreams, 171
defensive suspiciousness, 209
delusions, 257
displacement, 254
dominance, 206
dreams, 171
drive, 35
  aesthetic, 58
  anger, 66
  breathing, 43
  emergency, 62
  exercise, 46
  exploratory, 57
  fear, 64
  hunger, 40
  inter-relations of, 73

INDEX

drive – *contd*
parental, 49
security, 53
sex, 48
sleep, 44

ego; the self as an active agent
(=I)
ego adjustment, 248–59
ego control, 212
ego drive, 211
ego involvement, 126: the degree
to which, in any behaviour,
the person feels that his
reputation (self-sentiment)
is at stake
electronic computer, 148
environment, 194
ethology, 59: the study of animal
behaviour in natural setting
euphoria, 215: a mood of happiness or the personality
trait distinguished by a tendency to this response
excitement, 70, 200

factor analysis, 185
factors, 184
fantasy satisfaction, 252
fear and hope, 98
feedback, 71
figure-ground, 141
fluency, 192
focussing, 156
free association, 139

general emotionality, 199
genital stage, 235
gestalt, 149: a configuration
which forms a unified whole
and has properties which

are not found in any of its
parts, e.g., a musical pattern

halo effect, 199
hate, 112
heredity, 194
hypothesis, 174: a suggested
explanation of a complex set
of data

identification, 252: the process
by which a person allies
himself with another in
such a way as to regard the
pains and satisfactions of
this other as equivalent to
his own, e.g., boy identifies
with father and boasts of
father's achievements
imagery, 167
incubation, 173: with regard to
thinking, a period of no
conscious attention to the
problem but during which
unconscious processes are
operating towards its solution
individual differences, 181
inhibition, 82
innate grouping effect, 142
innate perceptual factors, 139
intelligence, 183
interposition, 157
introversion, 207: the tendency
to direct attention inwards
rather than outwards; the
term is used in varied ways.
See text
I.Q., 182

kindliness, 205

264

FOR THE BEST IN PAPERBACKS, LOOK FOR THE

A CHOICE OF PENGUINS AND PELICANS

Adieux Simone de Beauvoir

This 'farewell to Sartre' by his life-long companion is a 'true labour of love' (the *Listener*) and 'an extraordinary achievement' (*New Statesman*).

British Society 1914–45 John Stevenson

A major contribution to the Pelican Social History of Britain, which 'will undoubtedly be the standard work for students of modern Britain for many years to come' – *The Times Educational Supplement*

The Pelican History of Greek Literature Peter Levi

A remarkable survey covering all the major writers from Homer to Plutarch, with brilliant translations by the author, one of the leading poets of today.

Art and Literature Sigmund Freud

Volume 14 of the Pelican Freud Library contains Freud's major essays on Leonardo, Michelangelo and Dostoevsky, plus shorter pieces on Shakespeare, the nature of creativity and much more.

A History of the Crusades Sir Steven Runciman

This three-volume history of the events which transferred world power to Western Europe – and founded Modern History – has been universally acclaimed as a masterpiece.

A Night to Remember Walter Lord

The classic account of the sinking of the *Titanic*. 'A stunning book, incomparably the best on its subject and one of the most exciting books of this or any year' – *The New York Times*

FOR THE BEST IN PAPERBACKS, LOOK FOR THE 🐧

A CHOICE OF PENGUINS AND PELICANS

The Literature of the United States Marcus Cunliffe

The fourth edition of a masterly one-volume survey, described by D. W. Brogan in the *Guardian* as 'a very good book indeed'.

The Sceptical Feminist Janet Radcliffe Richards

A rigorously argued but sympathetic consideration of feminist claims. 'A triumph' – *Sunday Times*

The Enlightenment Norman Hampson

A classic survey of the age of Diderot and Voltaire, Goethe and Hume, which forms part of the Pelican History of European Thought.

Defoe to the Victorians David Skilton

'Learned and stimulating' (*The Times Educational Supplement*). A fascinating survey of two centuries of the English novel.

Reformation to Industrial Revolution Christopher Hill

This 'formidable little book' (Peter Laslett in the *Guardian*) by one of our leading historians is Volume 2 of the Pelican Economic History of Britain.

The New Pelican Guide to English Literature Boris Ford (ed.)
Volume 8: The Present

This book brings a major series up to date with important essays on Ted Hughes and Nadine Gordimer, Philip Larkin and V. S. Naipaul, and all the other leading writers of today.